The Journey to my Life Purpose

The Journey to my Life Purpose

by Elizabeth Ann

CONSCIOUS CARE PUBLISHING PTY LTD

The Journey to my Life Purpose

Copyright © 2015 by Elizabeth Ann. All rights reserved.

First Published 2015 by: Conscious Care Publishing Pty Ltd
PO Box 776, Rockingham, WA 6968, Australia
Phone: (61+) 1300 814 115   www.consciouscarepublishing.com

First Edition printed August 2015.

Notice of Rights
This book is sold subject to the condition that it shall not, by way of trade or otherwise, be lent, resold, hired out, or otherwise circulated without the publisher's prior consent, in any form of binding or cover, other than that in which it is published, and without a similar condition, including this condition being imposed on the subsequent purchaser. All rights reserved by the publisher. No part of this publication may be reproduced, stored in a retrieval system, or transmitted in any form, or by any means, electronic, digital, mechanical, photocopying, scanning, recorded or otherwise, without the prior written permission of the copyright owner. Requests to the copyright owner should be addressed to Permissions Department, Conscious Care Publishing Pty Ltd, PO Box 776, Rockingham, WA 6968, Australia,
Phone: (61+) 300 814 115 or email admin@consciouscarepublishing.com

Categories
1. Self Help. 2. New Age. 3. Mind, Body, Spirit

Limits of Liability/Disclaimer of Warranty:
While the publisher and author have used their best efforts in preparing this book, they make no representations or warranties with respect to the accuracy or completeness of the contents of this book and specifically disclaim any implied warranties of merchantability or fitness for a particular purpose. No warranty may be created or extended by sales representatives or written sales materials. The author of this book does not dispense medical advice or prescribe the use of any technique as a form of treatment for physical, emotional, or medical problems without the advice of a physician, either directly or indirectly. The advice and strategies contained herein may not be suitable for your situation. You should consult with a professional where appropriate. The intent of the author is only to offer information for a general nature to help you in your request for a happier life. Neither the publisher nor author shall be liable for any loss of profit or any other commercial damages, including but not limited to special, incidental, consequential, or other damages. The author and the publisher assume no responsibility for your actions.

Conscious Care Publishing publishes in a variety of print and electronic format and by print-on-demand. Some material included with standard print versions of this book may not be included in e-books or in print-on-demand. If this book refers to media such as a CD or DVD that is not included in the version you purchased, you may download this material at www.consciouscarepublishing.com

National Library of Australia Cataloguing-in-Publication entry:
Author: Ann, Elizabeth, 1949-
The Journey to my Life Purpose / by Liz Atherton
ISBN 9780987409768 (Paperback), 9780987409775 (Digital)
Ann, Elizabeth, 1949-
Smith, Peter, Cover Illustrator.
Rocky Hudson, Editor

Printed by Lightning Source
Typeset & cover design by Conscious Care Publishing Pty Ltd
158.1
ISBN: 978-0-9874097-6-8

*From my heart to yours
on your spiritual journey*

Contents

Introduction

PART ONE
Chapter 1 ~ 0-19 years appoximately	1
Chapter 2 ~ Marriage and children	9
Chapter 3 ~ Moving across the world 37-53 years	25
Chapter 4 ~ Spiritual growth 43-57 years	39
Chapter 5 ~ Overcoming problems 57-59 years	53
Chapter 6 ~ Enjoying later life	69
Chapter 7 ~ My personal history	77

PART TWO
Chapter 8 ~ Keeping a journal	93
Chapter 9 ~ Numerology	99
Chapter10 ~ Meditation	109
Chapter 11 ~ Reflexology	115
Chapter 12 ~ Psychic readings	119
Chapter 13 ~ Reiki healing	129
Chapter 14 ~ The end of my journey	131

Further information	135
About the author	137
Acknowledgements	139

Introduction

This book is being written for all those people who have a desire to go on a spiritual journey.

It will give you some insight in to how the journey can stop and start (in other words might take one step forward and three steps back), but when you reach awareness and have found the joy and passion in your heart – then you have reached the place you need to be. This book will also help those who want to integrate a professional career with their spiritual journey. I do hope you will all be inspired and go forth in spite of the pitfalls in life.

By telling you my story, I am hoping that you can resonate with the feelings I have had, and help yourself with the tools and tips I have given to you in the self-help section.

We are all born into this world with a life's purpose, and if we take time to come out of the mind and into the heart and gut feeling, we can find enlightenment and purpose in our lives. This can be truly done with positivity in your lives and regular meditation.

By looking at life in a positive way instead of having negative thoughts constantly, we can turn our minds around, and feel good about ourselves in every respect.

I do hope you as a reader of this book learn something which you can use in your daily lives!

Good Luck to everyone on your special journey to your life purpose!

Love, Light and Blessings to you all.

Elizabeth Ann.

Part one

A memoir of my life

- CHAPTER 1 -

0-19 *Years Approximately*

I was born on the first day of June 1949, being the second child of four. I have a brother, who is four years older, and two sisters, one two years younger and the other four years younger than me. I have no personal recollection of what happened during the first two years of my life.

At the age of 3 years I remember living in a bungalow, which is a single storey house, and that was in a place called Staines in Middlesex, UK. My Aunty Wendy came to visit

The Journey to my Life Purpose

us quite regularly, and she was a policewoman. The sight of her uniform always frightened me at this age. Also at this age my younger sister was a baby of one year old and my older brother was at school and he was 7 years old.

At 4 years old, I used to walk to the local shops for a loaf of bread for my mum, and thought they were a very long way from my house. I went back on a visit years later and found the shops were only a few steps away! At this age I remember my mum asking me to collect eggs from the chickens we kept at the end of the garden. I felt quite responsible being asked to do this job!!

We moved house from Staines in the south of England to the north of England, to a place called Keighley in Yorkshire. My dad started a new job as a Primary School Teacher. I was not impressed with my new surroundings. My youngest sister was born just before we moved house, and she was four months old when we moved to Keighley. Our house in Keighley was a big Victorian house with four storeys to it. It had a cellar where my mum did all the family washing on a Monday. The cellar housed a copper top washing machine and an old-fashioned ringer. My mum took all day doing the washing – very different from today!! We also lived over a park – called Victoria Park – and this is where they had circuses; town galas; and fairs, with roundabouts, kiss me

0-19 Years approximately

quick hats, and all manner of things to catch your eye – which was great as a small child. Each year all these events happened in the park and my sisters and I had much fun meeting all the people who came with the circuses and fairs!!

At 5 years old I started school, going with my dad on the bus as we didn't have a car in those days (1950's). My school was quite a journey from my house and so I didn't have a lot of friends from my neighbourhood going to the same school. On my first day at school I remember having trouble with the zip on my raincoat – it seemed such a difficult task for me!!

At the age of 6 ½ years I became very ill and it seemed that my mum, dad, family and the family doctor didn't seem to know what was wrong with me. I remember my mum was not very happy with me when I started to be sick, as I had gone outside playing in the pouring rain in a cotton dress and it was very cold weather!! My Mum and family worried about me for about a week, especially my younger sisters, who thought I was going to die! I was very oblivious to all of this, as I was too sick to know what was going on.

Eventually it was decided that I needed to go into hospital as my doctor was worried that I might be contagious. Upon

The Journey to my Life Purpose

entering the local hospital I was placed in an isolation room, and had no contact with other children or adults. It seemed like ages before they found out that I had pneumonia, and it took me several weeks to get better. I remember it being a very lonely existence in hospital at that age, but I was well looked after by the nurses. When I arrived home, I was so relieved to see my family, and it made me realise how fortunate I had been to come through my ordeal!! My sisters and brother were very kind to me for a few days, but after a while sisterly and brotherly love got back to normal!

My mother sent me to the hospital for sunray treatment to help me build up my immune system. I had to go there twice a week – I guess that was the thing they seemed to do way back in the fifties!

As my time progressed at Ingrow Primary School in Keighley I was able to go on the bus with Freda, the girl next door to us. She was rather a bully and tended to show off, so I didn't really get along with her very well.

When I was 8 years old my dad got a promotion to a new school. My teacher didn't like this and tried to victimize me in class. Mum and dad moved me and my younger sister to a new school, Riddlesden Primary School, which was so much better and I made some good friends.

0-19 Years approximately

At the age of 9 years I achieved first prize for handwriting in a competition run by Brooke Bond tea for schools in the whole of the UK, and won a cookery book worth seven shillings and sixpence.

I sat my 11+ examinations – these determine which kind of high school you will attend. At this age I learnt Scottish country dancing, which I enjoyed very much. Dad moved to another new position as Headmaster at a primary school in Hebden Bridge, Yorkshire – so we moved house and I left Riddlesden Primary School. I started the new school where Dad is Headmaster – I didn't like it. It was really hard being at the same school where your father is Headmaster. All the kids seemed to think you had preferential treatment, which I hasten to add "was not the case".

The great thing was that I only had to be at my dad's school for one term, and then I was transferred at 12 years old to a senior comprehensive school, called Calder High School. This school was the first comprehensive school in the UK, so it was very much a venture into a new way of learning. I seemed to settle quite well as I found that if you achieved a higher grade in some subjects you were placed higher up in your year, so I feel it helped you achieve things you enjoy! For instance I was always pretty good at English, so I went up to higher classes in my year for that, but I was not very

The Journey to my Life Purpose

good at mathematics so stayed in the same class for this.

Also at this time in my life we lived in the Vicarage – the reason being that we were unable to find a house so we applied for a rental accommodation. The local vicar, who was on the Council, had plenty of space for a family at his Vicarage, so he invited us to live with him. We end up staying there for four years. We lived in the little village called Mytholmroyd, and I become very involved with church activities such as choir and amateur dramatics. Between the ages of 13 and 15 I had quite a lot of involvement with acting, singing, dancing, and stage make-up, and enjoyed being involved with stage musicals such as Oliver Twist, Carousel, My Fair Lady, and The Sound of Music, which was all good fun!

I was also an avid Beatles fan, along with my sisters. We managed to cover the walls of two bedrooms in the vicarage with an array of Beatle pictures. I hasten to add that my mother kept saying, "If another of these Beatle pictures goes on the wall – I will take the lot down!". We always put a small one up so she didn't notice!!

At the age of 15 years my dad was promoted again to a position as Headmaster of a primary school in Hertfordshire in the South of England. I started yet another school, for the last year of my schooling. I found it very hard to learn and fit in, and I also found it hard to catch up, the result being that I failed my exams!

Upon leaving school at 16 I was hoping to continue to redo my 'O' levels at college, but I found it was a hard task with all the moves I had had. After having an assessment at a local college, I decided to go and work as Jr. Clerk at the Hertfordshire County Council offices and learn typing and shorthand at Ware College in Hertfordshire during Day Release from work.

My other siblings were getting on with their lives; my older brother, at 20 years old, was working with Telecommunications and studying also – so he was doing what was known as a Sandwich Course! My younger sisters were still at school. My mother at this time was now back at work, after having been at home for a number of years. She worked as a secretary at a very big pharmaceutical company in the town where we lived in Hertfordshire. All the changes in schools whilst I was growing up had quite an impact on my confidence, which sometimes affected my ability to achieve different things in my life. At this age I felt a little unsure of my ability, and this tended to make me feel very shy and withdrawn. I also found it hard to talk to boys, so I did not have many boyfriends at this time in my life.

The Journey to my Life Purpose

When I was 18 years old, I joined a group named 18+. It was for young people between the ages of 18 and 30 years. This I felt gave me the confidence I needed, and soon after I joined the club in Hertford, I became involved in arranging a lot of activities. My social life started to take off and I enjoyed the company of very good friends.

Also at this age I changed jobs a few times within the secretarial field, as I sought to find my niche.

At 19 years I met my first serious boyfriend, Robin — my first love. This didn't last long — about three months — as we had very different views on life. I also found a new job in London at British Petroleum, a company which looked after their employees very well, and I stayed there for eight years.

- CHAPTER 2 -

Marriage and Children

At 20 years I passed my driving test and I also met my second serious love, Mick. We got engaged after six months, but this only lasted a year, as again we were very different in all aspects. While still going out with Mick, I decided to go to Jersey for a holiday with a girlfriend. This holiday helped me with my decision to leave him – this was a very good decision, but of course I didn't realise this until I met my husband in 1971.

The Journey to my Life Purpose

In September 1971, whilst I was still going out with Mick, my younger sister decided to emigrate to Perth Australia to join her boyfriend Kevin and his family. She was engaged to him and my parents were not too happy about this, as she was only 19 years old! Anyway they made a decision to let her go, but she had to stay in Australia for two years before she could return. My mum, dad and I went to Southampton to see her off with many farewell tears. Of course my sister didn't envisage meeting another guy on board, and having a relationship, so when she came to meet her fiancé in Perth, she really found she had made a huge mistake! Therefore, she was in Perth W.A. with nobody she knew, because Kevin's family disowned her, as she wasn't going to marry him. Incidentally, the guy on board went to Melbourne and she didn't see him again. She later (in 1973) married her Western Australian husband.

At 21 years I had a beautiful coming of age party at home with family, friends and my fiancé Mick. In August of that year Mick broke off the engagement, which initially devastated me, but I quickly pulled myself together and took a holiday with my friend Barbara, to Majorca, Spain. At this time I also found my job in human resources at British Petroleum had become so interesting, and my boss helped me to gain a lot confidence by letting me do other things in my work, such as interviewing candidates for the

Marriage and Children

company and setting up workshops for graduates entering the company. This was more interesting than being a secretary. Interestingly, at this time I shared an office with other secretaries and the jealousy among these girls was quite profound – I did not allow this to get in the way of my career development.

I took a holiday in September 1971, with my girlfriend Ruth, to Dubrovinik in Yugoslavia. Yugoslavia is now called Serbia and Croatia, as the war in the early 90s divided the country. At the time I went it was a communist country, and although the streets of Dubrovinik were covered in marble, the shops I noticed didn't have many luxurious items. It was a beautiful holiday, full of history, and the town of Dubrovnik had a wall around it, to protect it from outside predators it seemed! I guess it had been used as a fortress in years gone by. I met a lot of German people there, and that made me feel I would like to learn the language, so I went to night classes for a few sessions when I returned home, but quickly realised it was not my forte – languages!

In November 1971 I meet my husband-to-be. I was introduced to him by a girlfriend called Sue, and she was in a serious relationship with my husband's brother. She wanted me to go on a blind date, as a foursome, and it was to be to the yearly graduation ball at a teachers' training

The Journey to my Life Purpose

college. I said okay, so long as if it didn't work out she would not be upset! She actually pointed him out to me at an 18+ club event, the week before the blind date, and I thought it was another guy who had a bald head. I said "in no uncertain terms" that I would not go out with him: "He's not my type." This just shows how, at that age, looks seem to be so important!!

Of course when the following Saturday arrived and we were introduced, I was so shocked that he wasn't bald after all, and I had the best time with him – I don't think we stopped talking all evening. Unbeknown to me, at the end of the evening, his brother offered him the car keys to his red MGB car to take me home. I thought, gosh he's a good catch – a great car as well!! Little knowing that he had no car and he was borrowing his brother's to impress me. From that start, we have gone through the trials and tribulations of 42 years of marriage, and had three beautiful girls and three grandchildren – two boys and girl! My husband and I enjoyed a very happy time together in the seven months since we met, and then I went for another holiday, to Corfu in Greece with my girlfriend Linda. I had already booked this holiday before I met up with my husband, so did not want to let my friend Linda down. Linda also had a new boyfriend, so we both thought it would be a good idea to go along with our plan and see if we missed our boyfriends

Marriage and Children

while we were away. I wrote several letters to Peter and missed him terribly, but Linda enjoyed the advances of all the Greek men. I was a bit dubious of them, but she enjoyed the catch!! We had a beautiful holiday seeing quite a few sights by boat, and travelling on the ramshackle buses. As I look back on these holidays I had while young, I realise that it was important that I had those experiences then, as after I was married there were not many trips abroad, due to financial commitments.

Upon my return to the UK from Corfu, I was greeted enthusiastically by Peter, and we then decided to get engaged in July 1972. Incidentally the same happened to Linda, and she married in November 1972. Peter and I married in February 1973. I moved jobs to BP Harlow, which was a wrong move, so I moved back to the London office. The first flat we lived in was rented accommodation in Stansted, Essex. This was a 16th century one-bedroom place with oak beams, and everything was on a slant. Our first family dinner to entertain our parents was quite a hoot – I had made "Duck à l'orange" with all the trimmings – I took the duck out of the oven to test it for being cool, and dropped it onto the slanted floor. It slid across, I picked it up, washed it under the tap, and placed it in the oven for another quick cook. I hasten to add that everyone said it was the best "Duck à l'orange" that they ever had tasted –

The Journey to my Life Purpose

little did they know!!! We had many happy times there and I commuted to the BP office in London from the railway station across the road from the flat – how convenient was that! We also met some beautiful friends who we are still in contact with to this day!

In 1974, we moved to Harlow Essex, as we were on a list for council flats in order to save for our own house.

In that year we went to a huge concert in Watford Football Club stadium, where Elton John was showing. My husband agreed to let me climb on his shoulders to see the event – wouldn't happen now!!

On New Year's Eve 1974 my dear uncle John, my mother's twin brother, died of a heart attack in the chair in his front room. This happened after going to a New Year's Eve party – what a way to go for him, but a terrible shock for his family – his wife and three teenage children. His mother (my grandma) died the year before, and my mum said he never got over it. Uncle John was very much a clown – he was always making everyone laugh but underneath I think he was a very sad man! We all missed him terribly!!

In the summer of 1975 we moved into a new house in Newport Essex, and we enjoyed decorating and buying

Marriage and Children

furniture for our new home. We started to meet a lot of young couples who lived in the village, and I commuted by train to London for my job with BP.

The following year in 1976 we enjoyed a wonderful relaxing holiday on the Isle of Wight with great friends – we did this for two years running. In November 1976 I found out I was expecting our first baby. The job I was in at BP was rather stressful, and I had a threatened miscarriage, so the company put me on sick leave. When I returned to work after Christmas and New Year 1977, it was suggested that I take on a more relaxed secretarial role, and this suited me very well with commuting to London. In April 1977 I left BP after eight years of service, with lots of good wishes from my friends and workmates.

On fifth of July 1977 our first child was born at Princess Alexandra Hospital in Harlow, Essex. She weighed in at 7 lbs 15 oz – breach birth – bottom first, naturally – ouch!! A lovely baby, very good – I enjoyed being Mum to Louise. She was christened at three months, in the local church. My younger sister and her husband from Western Australia came to visit for the christening. We had lots of family and friends for the christening and it was a very enjoyable day. Louise enjoyed a toddler group we joined in the village of Newport, and she loved the interaction with many children

The Journey to my Life Purpose

around her age.

In 1979 I turned 30 years old, and for some reason I felt quite old. My husband was given a relocation with his job in British Oxygen, so we moved to Milton Keynes in Buckinghamshire. After settling into a new house I found that I was pregnant, and the pregnancy seemed to have its ups and downs. When I was four months pregnant, we went on a family holiday to North Devon with friends. We stayed on a farm and Louise enjoyed the sheep and lambs that were being born. I was finding it hard to walk up very steep cobbled hills, and it was not until we returned home that they let us know that my blood test, which was done before we went away, was a little bit in the grey zone. They said over the phone that I was likely to be expecting a spina bifida baby, and did I want to terminate this pregnancy? I exclaimed that I had had an awful lot movement for a spina bifida baby! I hasten to add we didn't sleep for a few nights, before I insisted that I needed an appointment for an ultrasound scan.

We had to drive 16 miles to the nearest hospital in Aylesbury to have the scan, and I had to drink 2 Litres of water on the journey. When we got there I was beside myself with worry! My husband said don't worry we can always have a German shorthaired pointer dog! Okay, typical male answer to

Marriage and Children

everything!!

I was seen pretty quickly and they started to investigate what was happening in my womb! I didn't dare look at the screen for fear of what I may find, but said many prayers at the same time. Guess what, they had tested for one baby, and there were two babies – one lying behind the other. What a shock, eh! My husband came into the room and was so surprised to say the least, and Louise my eldest daughter thought it was great – she was jumping for joy – someone for her to play with!

The pregnancy progressed to Christmas 1980, and then I started to dilate and they thought I was going to have the babies. So I was whisked into hospital to have a stitch in my cervix, so that I could keep them a bit longer. They were due February 20, 1981.

I was home for a few weeks from Christmas 1980 to January 1981, and then my blood pressure started to rise, so I had to be in hospital until I had my babies on 9 February 1981; two little girls, Amy and Julia. Amy was 6 lbs 11 oz (head first), Julia was 6 lbs 6 oz (feet first) – both natural births and lovely babies, but such hard work with Louise a toddler.

At Christmas 1981 I decided to do an evening job sorting

The Journey to my Life Purpose

the post at the local post office, for extra money – little did I know it would interfere with my health.

In February 1982 I eventually realised I couldn't cope with no support, and fell into deep depression. This was not a good time in my life and I was very lucky to have a good doctor and health visitor, who arranged for various people to give me a support network. I initially had four days rest with my mum on my own, and then had to go back to my support network at home. Whilst I was away at Mum's, my mother-in-law and my husband helped to look after the little ones. On returning home my health visitor organised a Student Children's Nurse to come and help me with feeding, and nappy changing – this was a godsend! She also helped to babysit as the girls became older. I also had a nurse call on me to check how I was progressing once a week, and I was regularly checked by the doctor. Before I got the support, I remember going to see a psychologist at the local clinic, and he said, "If you don't manage to pull yourself out of this depression – we might have to put your children into care." This statement sent ringing bells in my ears, and I said to myself, Well Liz, you don't want that to happen! – so I made myself better – I believe the mind is a powerful thing, and I knew I just had to be strong and positive and prove to myself that I could do it!! From that day to this, sometimes if I feel myself going into that dark

Marriage and Children

tunnel again, I quickly look at all the positive things in my life and I can bring my life back on track!! I also need to mention to all those who are reading this who have suffered depression, it isn't always easy to go through this, and at times I would have days when I still couldn't cope, but I guess I had to make it work as I had three little children depending on me!! Also, even in that time, in the early 80s, I was given a long playing record by my doctor, and it had instructions on "How to Meditate". He told me to allow 15 minutes each day to meditate and relax. I found that I began to yearn for that time to relax, and this helped me to become much better in myself. I still do meditation and I honestly think it is a wonderful way of de-stressing the body, along with my Reiki healing.

In 1983 I experienced the early stages of menopause and of course there was not a lot of medication to help with it in the UK at that time. All medication was still being researched, so was not freely given out to the public. I also found my depression seemed to be worse in the winter months in the UK, and I heard about a condition called "Seasonal Affective Disorder", or "SAD".

In the July of 1983 we decided to have a family holiday in Bournemouth, Hants. This was a lovely holiday with the children, even though we were stretched to the limit with

The Journey to my Life Purpose

chasing those lively two-year-olds on the beach, and coping with an inquisitive six-year-old who wanted to know the answer to every question at the most awkward moments. Such as "where do babies come from?", while you are trying to stop two-year-old twins running in opposite directions!!

In 1984 I seemed to have more time and the girls are growing up. Their ages were three for the twins and six for my eldest daughter. My eldest daughter was full-time at primary school and enjoyed going to Brownies in the UK. The twins were also at nursery school every morning, so I started a part-time job for a few hours a week. The job was helping with administrative work for teachers of English as a second language, and it also helped to keep my brain ticking over. In the school summer holidays we took a week's holiday to Bournemouth again, and it seemed much less stressful this year. The owner of our guesthouse agreed to babysit for us, and we started to have more time out together as husband and wife.

In 1985 my sister arrived for a holiday from Australia. My husband and I had been doing five jobs between us, and feeling that we were not making headway financially, or having any quality of life, so we had a discussion with her, regarding life in Perth, Western Australia. She gave us a lot of hope to move, and really to form a good life for our

Marriage and Children

family in Perth, but didn't try to make our minds up for us. We had to do that! It was a little hard as we could not afford to go for a holiday. My sister and her husband sent us magazines, newspapers and tapes of what life was like there. We then made an application to Australia House. This application seemed to take forever, but we were determined to go through with it, as our quality of life depended on it. We also said it had to work for us as there was no giving up and coming back.

We started our application in late 1985 and had our first interview with Australia House in March 1986. In the summer of 1986 we put our house up for sale, but had a lot of trouble trying to sell it as the property market was not very good. England was in a financial depression and houses were not selling, as people could not afford to buy. Australia House sent us a letter in September 1986, which said, "if you are not able to sell your house by November 1986 we will have to forgo your application". I sent a begging letter to them asking for an extension – they gave us until February 1987.

Whilst washing up one day in my kitchen I had an idea! I decided to put an advertisement in the local paper. It read: "If you wish to buy our house for £50,000 you can also have our beautiful Ford Sierra car for free." This was granted as a

The Journey to my Life Purpose

very good idea, and the local newspaper decided to make a front page spread with a photo of our house and car superimposed on my husband's hands! It did the trick, and we had loads of people come to see our house! The people who bought it didn't want our car, so we were able to sell that separately. The house was sold and we were able to leave the UK for Australia. We packed up and left our house just before Christmas and spent our last Christmas with family, before flying to Australia. This was a very enjoyable time with my family, and it seemed very apt to have Christmas before we left!

On January 2, 1987 we were taken by my mum and dad to Heathrow Airport. We flew out with Singapore airlines, and all our family and friends came to see us off. This was a very emotional farewell but also a very positive one, as it was an adventure that we would never forget! The weather flying out of Heathrow was pretty bleak, and of course we had hardly got out of UK airspace, when one of my darling daughters locked herself in the toilet! After much coaxing and cajoling we managed to get her to open the door! The journey seemed to be very long, especially as we had three young children – but when I look back, we took it all in our stride! My youngest daughter had the right idea as regards not eating too much – she drank plenty of orange juice, a few snacks and sweets – she was well all the way. The other

Marriage and Children

two children ate everything they could and were sick most of the way!

The Journey to my Life Purpose

- CHAPTER 3 -

Moving across the World 37 – 53 years

When we arrived in Perth Australia on the fourth of January 1987 at 2 am, we were met by my sister, husband and friends. They had come in two cars to transport us and all our belongings to my sister's house in East Fremantle. My sister's husband wanted to give us a guided tour of Perth, but we can't remember what we were supposed to see at 2 am in the morning.

When we arrived there was a big sailing celebration in

The Journey to my Life Purpose

Fremantle –"The America's Cup Defense". At that time there were no rental properties to be had as a lot of American visitors were in Fremantle for the America's Cup. So we had to stay at my sister's place for about six weeks, which was quite hard for us both. We decided to look for a house to buy – it took us six weeks to find something – which was quite good. We moved into our first house in a suburb called Samson, Western Australia on 14 February 1987.

At first it was a bit unsettling but after six months and deciding to buy a home of our own, so that we could put our roots down so to speak, we were very pleasantly surprised! We did of course miss family in England when it came to Christmas and birthdays, but we had my sister here, and also had started to make some very good friends!!

My husband found work here extremely quickly, as his skill as a design draughtsman was well sought after in the mining industry of Western Australia.

Of course when we moved into the house at Samson we didn't have much furniture, as we were still waiting for our furniture from the UK. We were very lucky to borrow some furniture from my sister's friends and bought new beds.

We did have some mishaps with one daughter, who had

Moving across the world 37 – 53 years

very fair skin. She had to be covered in sunscreen, and wear long sleeved T-shirts and a big hat. Whilst we were waiting to move into the house the girls went to a water playground as part of the summer holiday excursion in a playgroup for the school holidays. I dropped them off with the organisers and told them to keep the fair-skinned child covered and wearing plenty of sunscreen. When I picked her up with her sisters at 5:30 pm that day she was like a beetroot! I am afraid to say I flew into a rage at the organisers, and was told "we can't watch them all!" I took her to the doctor and he had to cut her clothes off, and she had second-degree burns! We plastered her in calamine lotion and put gauze on her burns. She was lucky, we didn't have any idea how the sun here could be! This was definitely a lesson to be learned from that day. To this day my daughter never sits in the sun! She and her partner have the same sort of skin, and when they go abroad to Phuket or Vietnam they do sightseeing not sun bathing!

Living in our new house I managed to settle little by little as time went on. I must admit I had a few homesick days. Living in Australia was very different from the UK. I know we speak the same language, but some of the ways of living, and the reaction to certain ways of doing things was hard to understand. My first encounter trying to fit in with mums at the local school gates was very different. Most of the mums

The Journey to my Life Purpose

jumped in their cars, and I didn't seem to meet people. I did join a group of mums who had a get-together by way of a coffee morning. I was asked to "take a plate" to the get-together. Of course I took a plate – little knowing that I was supposed to put something on the plate. Of course it was always remembered what I did, Ha! Ha!

After about six months of putting the house together, and seeing the girls settled at the local primary school, I decided, after buying myself a little white Mini, to find myself a job. This I felt would help me to settle into my life in Australia, and give me more purpose in my life. I went along to Boans Department store in Fremantle and asked for a job in retail. I think they liked my approach, since I'd been upfront with what I wanted, so I got the job! I was enrolled in a course to understand everything about the company, and to master the art of using a computerised till. Also, customer service was another aspect of learning about the rules and regulations of the job. I stayed at Boans in Fremantle for about six months, and then I decided that retail shop assistant work was not for me, and I felt I needed to utilise the secretarial skills I had. I also felt I needed to have a part-time position, as the children were still only young and new to Australia. So I found a position near home at a car yard, and the hours I worked were 8 till 12 noon Monday to Friday. The work was varied, but I found

Moving across the world 37 – 53 years

it a bit different from the secretarial work I did in the UK. One day I was stopped by the General Manager as I was answering calls on the reception in the Service Department. He said to me to not waste time giving a long spiel on the phone to customers – like, for instance, "Good morning, the company name and how can I help you"; he said just say "hello". I found this very hard to do, as people didn't know if they had the right phone number or not. I tried to follow what he said at first, but in the end I just continued as I had always done. Most people were happy with that. I stayed at the car yard for two years and then moved on to a few temporary positions.

In 1989 our whole family became Australian Citizens, and had a ceremony at the Fremantle Town Hall. To celebrate, my sister and her husband made a typical Australian barbecue lunch, with damper bread, and Pavlova for desert.

Also in 1989, we celebrated our 40th birthdays with friends and family at the Chalet Healy Hotel in the Perth hills. We all enjoyed the 60s dress-up night, which included a meal, rock 'n' roll music and transport in a London bus home. I dressed up in a Cilla Black wig, with a 50s rock 'n' roll dress, and my husband dressed up as a hippie with sunglasses and a long black wig. Most of the fellas dressed like this, as I guess most of them related to the hippie era in the late 60s.

The Journey to my Life Purpose

All in all this was a very enjoyable birthday and a good time was had by all!

At this time, we also built the swimming pool in the backyard. This was perfect timing, as the girls were the right age to enjoy this. The only thing was that I didn't swim; although I did go for swimming lessons, I didn't seem to have the confidence to actually swim.

During this period my husband decided to take a contract down south at a place called Capel, south of Bunbury. He decided to work away from home all week and come home at the weekends. This caused some inharmonious relations with our marriage, as he did not always understand the things that happened with the family whilst he had been away. It created friction between me and him, and also unsettled the family dynamics. We managed to have a holiday at a Caravan Park in Bunbury, during the school summer holidays, so that we could be as a family once more. My husband also joined a running group in Bunbury and we met all the members. We also stayed with some of the members and become good friends. These people then came up to our house in Samson and they enjoyed staying the weekend for pool parties. We started to have much more family time and things seemed to get back on track with family life.

Moving across the world 37 – 53 years

After four years away from home my husband finally decided to come back to Perth to work, and started a job in Kwinana, at Alcoa, in the drawing office as Section Leader. Very shortly after that, I secured a job at the Fremantle Cemetery board as a Funeral Memorial Clerk. This new position gave me a great deal of variety, including giving people grief counselling both on the phone and face-to-face. I worked at the cemetery for three years and gained a lot of experience – I also felt after working there that I had the ability to work anywhere I was employed. Because of this experience I became aware of spirituality!!!

I started to look into meditation classes, with a girlfriend who lived nearby. I also learned all about the benefits of aromatherapy oils, which I burned in the office of the Cemetery. The customers who come into the office enjoyed the relaxing aromas, and commented that it made them feel good, and helped them with their grief. My boss at the cemetery was not impressed with the burning of the oils, and tried hard to place negativity on the practice. This caused some friction, so I tried not to burn them whilst he was around. Whilst I was working at the Cemetery I had one day off each week, so I did a beauty course in West Perth. I learned Swedish massage, which I loved, waxing, facials and nails. The massage was the only thing I seemed to relate to, and I find I use this with my healing business

The Journey to my Life Purpose

even now.

In July 1990 my elder brother and his family come for a three week holiday. We showed them around Perth and they seemed to enjoy themselves. My brother and his family were in actual fact making Perth a stopover en route to their destination in the Great Barrier Reef in Queensland.

Whilst I was working at the Fremantle Cemetery from 1993 to 1996 I discovered the healing modality Reiki, through doing a workshop at an evening class in aromatherapy. It was a wonderful experience, taught by the lady who taught the aromatherapy techniques; she gave us a healing and this gave me a taste of the experience. It was not until I joined a yoga class that I came across a Reiki Master, namely the yoga teacher. I discovered the techniques of Reiki 1 from her, and went on to practice them on my friends and relatives.

After a few months I met another lady who was doing some Reiki sharing on a Sunday afternoon each month, so I became interested in this, and it made me much less anxious about my life. I then decided to learn Reiki 2, which enables you to be a practitioner and treat the public.

In 1994 we had several visitors from the UK come and see

Moving across the world 37 - 53 years

how we were settling down in Perth. We enjoyed showing people from the UK the lovely life we had managed to secure for ourselves, and they seemed very happy for us.

Also during this year I visited the UK for the first time in seven years. This was a very special visit as it was my mum and dad's 50th wedding anniversary. It seemed strange going back for a holiday, and I must admit I found it hard to settle down to life in the UK. I suddenly realised that my home is where my heart is, in Australia!! Life didn't seem to move on in England and the people were very negative – but I guess the weather has a lot to do with it – as most of the time they don't have sunshine! Much to the amazement of my family I had my suitcase packed a few days before I left. When I arrived back in Perth, I kissed the ground. I felt very pleased and blessed to be in the most beautiful place on earth, and still think that to this day!

In July 1995 we decided on an addition to our family – a Golden Retriever called Cleo. She was my eldest daughter's companion, while she did her extra studying after not passing her TEE exams first time around, we decided she could have a dog if she buckled down and passed her exams by redoing year 12 at North Lakes senior school. She came to the party and obtained good marks for University at Edith Cowan. She decided to do media and Aboriginal and

The Journey to my Life Purpose

intercultural studies.

In Christmas 1995 we decided to have a holiday in Denmark, W.A. with friends. This was like an English Christmas, as the temperature there was very similar – 15°C. Our eldest daughter went to her boyfriend's house for Christmas and had usual Perth temperatures – 35°C.

Cleo our dog was put into kennels whilst we were away, and the people at the kennels wished to breed from her. We had to ensure that she didn't go with any other dog, and they would pay for all expenses to ensure she had a good litter of puppies. She had five puppies, four males and one female, in February 1997. We brought one puppy, Oliver, home with her, much to Cleo's disgust. She (Cleo) takes a while to get used to having him around, and then they become inseparable.

In 2001, Cleo became quite ill, and we discovered she had lumps in her neck. It was found to be cancer of the lymph glands. We tried several alternative treatments, and then drugs to help her, but we lost her to the angels six months after the diagnosis. I eventually had to let her go. I took her to the vet and it was very hard to lift her into the car. When I saw the vet she would not let me take her home. I had to ring my daughter before I could make any decision. My

Moving across the world 37 – 53 years

daughter spoke to the vet and asked if there was any hope. The vet said "no", and it would be best for her to be put down. I went into another room as I couldn't watch what the vet had to do. Whilst I was in this room with my friend Cheryl all the other dogs in the waiting room started howling. I asked Cheryl, "What is happening?" She said they were all going out in sympathy with Cleo – I found this quite amazing that animals could sense if one of their own was dying!! I burst into tears and there was great sorrow around us at losing such a lovely dog. The vet was so good, she laid Cleo on a table with beautiful candles around her so that my daughters could come and visit her to say goodbye. We all did this as a family in the evening and we had closure. I have Cleo's ashes in the house to this day, along with those of her son Oliver, who died at the age of 11.

Whilst I was learning about Transactional Analysis for counselling clients, I was also working as a Medical Secretary in Sir Charles Gardiner Hospital in Perth. The hours were pretty long and I felt I needed a holiday, so I took my two eldest girls to the UK for a holiday to see my parents. We had a good time reminiscing about where we lived and seeing quite a few old friends. Before I went I was told by spirit to be careful travelling, and of course I didn't really take their advice as I wanted to have a holiday.

The Journey to my Life Purpose

The flight took us 26 hours via Brunei and Abu Dhabi, and my eldest daughter was strip-searched at Abu Dhabi, because her arms had been uncovered in transit. I was beside myself at the thought she was going to be whisked away never to be seen again. The relief was so overwhelming when she was returned to us – but of course there was no explanation by the authorities about why it had been done!! We arrived at Heathrow airport very tired and fraught, and were picked up by my wonderful dad, aged 79, who was a little perplexed as to where to find the parked car!! Eventually we found the car, but on subsequent trips to the UK, I decided I would use a coach from Heathrow, as it was much too much for my dear dad to handle!! As our holiday progressed we met up with different old friends, and one day we ventured into London and went on the London Eye to view the city. Whilst we were on the London Eye they stopped it, and we had to disembark! There was no explanation, but as we were travelling home that night on the train we looked at other passengers' newspapers, and there in print was news of the death defying attack on the skyscraper buildings of New York. It was 11 September 2001. At the time it had happened we were on the London Eye and that was supposed to be the next hit!! We were oblivious to all this, and when we returned home to my mum and dad they were so pleased we were safe. I really needed to listen to spirit a lot more, and asked them to

Moving across the world 37 – 53 years

forgive me, and keep us safe on the return journey home. Spirit told me "you are in safe hands – you are on a Muslim airline – they won't hurt their own". This was reassuring for me and my two girls, but I guessed we still had to be vigilant coming home. Again I kissed the ground here in Perth when I came home!!

The Journey to my Life Purpose

- CHAPTER 4 -

Spiritual Growth
43-57 years

In the late 90s, I joined a psychic development class which was run by a lady called Jackie Lindsay and her husband in Jarrahdale. This class was very informative and helped me to learn many aspects of spirituality along with like-minded people. Whilst doing this class I happened to mention that I'd been giving Reiki to cancer patients voluntarily, at the Cottage Hospice in Shenton Park, and felt rather nauseous and unwell whilst giving Reiki to the patients. I was told by Jackie that I would need another attunement if I wished

The Journey to my Life Purpose

to continue giving treatments, and that I also needed to ground myself more and protect myself. So, Jackie put me in touch with a lady called Valerie Deacon, who taught Reiki 1 and Reiki 2 classes by donation. I went to Val Deacon, then sat Reiki 1 again with a new Reiki attunement technique. A few weeks later I sat Reiki 2 again. What a difference, and no more feeling nauseous when treating clients. This was a great learning curve for me and made such a difference to my energy. From this time on I have felt my Reiki to be my purpose on my road to spirituality. It seems to have enhanced all of the modalities I have learnt, and works well alongside anything I have learnt in my life.

In 1997 I decided to do some counselling studies. This took me a few years, and I did it part-time whilst working as a Medical Secretary around the public hospitals in Perth. These counselling studies were run in Fremantle and Subiaco in the evenings. There were several Transactional Analysis modules to be completed, and they included working within the child in each one of us, the games people play, and spirituality, among others. These modules have all helped me to ascertain clients needs and wants, and taught me how to solve problems at the end of each session with clients. The counselling I studied was a form of Holistic Counselling, and it is certainly a good academic tool to have when dealing with a stressed client.

Spiritual growth 43-57 years

This I feel was the beginning of my experience with spirituality, and I was meeting some interesting people at this time of my life. I did feel my life was somewhat busy, with working full-time as a Medical Secretary, and having my teenage girls still at home. I was increasingly aware that I had to work in what I knew at this stage of my life, yet there was a yearning in my heart to follow my spiritual path. I knew it would happen, but I also knew it had to be at the right moment!!

In May 2003, I enrolled on a weekend course in Psychic Development. It was a very uplifting course and gave me a great deal of confidence to start my Reiki healing business part-time, whilst still working as a Medical Secretary part-time. While I was on this course I met a lady who was moving into a new house in Attadale, not far from my new house in Bicton. She had a spare room which she was willing to rent out to me at a very reasonable price. I started to heal some friends, and then other people, as news of my practice spread by word-of-mouth. The lady of the house went away for six weeks on holiday, and the business started to grow rapidly. When she returned, she was not happy with a few things I had done to create a more ambient environment for my clients. We had a disagreement and I ended up finding another place in Melville House, Palmyra. This was a very good opportunity for me and it enabled me to move on to

The Journey to my Life Purpose

the next step much more comfortably. I always feel small steps enable you to reach your goal in life!!

During this period I started to obtain spiritual messages from the feet and head of clients' bodies whilst doing Reiki healing. The messages came with such gusto that I was unable to keep them in my memory until the end of the healing. So I talked to my guides, and asked them to give me the messages at the end of each session, when I went to wash my hands. This worked very well indeed, and clients were so pleased that they had some answers to what had been bothering them! As I have progressed with my healings, I now have learnt to do automatic writing, at the end of each session, so the client has a written message to take away with them. Some of my clients have kept these messages, and they have said it helps them with their progress, especially if they came to see me with anxiety issues and depression. They also feel it helps them to become unstuck in their lives, and gives them more direction!

Another avenue I started looking into was further study. I did some short courses, which I felt would help me in my business in case I needed to take another direction. One of these courses was "Face Readings". I did this with a lady in Lesmurdie, and it took two days to learn. It has helped when doing my readings, as looking at people's faces helps

Spiritual growth 43-57 years

me to gain an understanding of their characteristics.

At the end of May 2005 I set up another healing room in Hamilton Hill to gain a different clientele to Melville. This proved to be unsuccessful. The reason it turned out that way was because of the location, and I found it was not as fruitful after all with regards to the workshops in the centre. The lady who owned the place, or perhaps rented it, led me to believe that it was a very busy business, yet after a month or two, I found that my clients did not want to travel out of Fremantle. I therefore decided it was a lesson learnt to stay in the Melville/Bicton area, where I lived, and to build up the clientele from there.

At this time also I went for an interview for a job in an old people's home in Redcliffe near the airport – this I felt would bring in extra funds for my business, but as it happened I didn't get the job. I felt spirit wanted me to be patient and not to look for other positions – the home business would grow, I had to trust in this!!! My clairvoyant and counsellor, Becky, actually told me that my business would be doing very well in five months' time, and that I should trust this more. It's something we all have to abide by – the trusting bit!

In April 2006 my healing business in the rooms I shared

The Journey to my Life Purpose

in Melville House started to take off. The room was extremely convenient to my house and I was able to nip home and have lunch in between clients. Also at this time my daughter had moved out of home and had gone to Esperance for help with her problems, which freed me up to follow my passion in life.

I also feel I should mention at this point in the book that my awareness and passion for what I did was solely my own. I tried to involve my husband but of course he was very skeptical on the matter. I feel it could help someone reading my book to realise partners do not always support you on your journey to spirituality, as they do not always have the same belief system as you!!! So in actual fact we need to look elsewhere to get the support we need, and to help with our belief system and awareness! We need to join spiritual churches or form groups which bring like-minded people to us for discussion and friendship, and to also feed the soul!!

Joining a few business networking groups helped me to gain confidence in my ability to trust that the business would materialise. It also gave me the insight to develop my self-worth, and to speak out about my passion, which in turn, helped others who came to me for healing and guidance. I must also stress that at this time I became very tuned into

Spiritual growth 43-57 years

spirit when I was healing, and I became the messenger to spirit in that I was able to transmit messages on to clients through automatic writing.

In June 2006 I started doing meditation workshops, initially from my friend Rikki's house in Palmyra, on the last Sunday of every month. Over the course of four years I ran these workshops in my house at Bicton, with sometimes as many as 22 people attending. The workshop always had a speaker, who would talk about different spiritual modalities. We started the workshop 2 pm on a Sunday afternoon with our meditation, and then we had a guest speaker for 30 minutes. Refreshments were given and I charged $15 per person.

These workshops helped me to speak with many spiritual people at different networking events I attended, and glean information on what they do. I also invited them to come along to my meditation workshop and sell their products or give out information. Each member of the workshop enjoyed learning a variety of different spiritual modalities, as well as how to meditate. There was also time to have refreshments and this gave everyone a chance to meet other spiritual people. These workshops were held from June 2006 until April 2010, when we moved from Bicton. All of these workshops were a very good experience for my clients, and they told me that it helped them to

The Journey to my Life Purpose

grow spiritually by asking questions, and obtaining valid information about things they didn't always find in books. I do feel that this idea of having a meditation group helped me to gain confidence in teaching others in Reiki, and also becoming a marriage celebrant later on in my life. The meditation group ran along these lines – firstly everyone arrived in dribs and drabs from 1:55 pm – 2:10 pm on the last Sunday of every month except December and January. We started the guided meditation at 2:15 pm and if anyone turned up late they had to wait in the next room until we had finished, as this disturbed some members. Also whilst we meditated my dog Oliver used to either snore or try to lick people in the early days. He had to learn it was not appropriate to do that, or else he had to go outside. He quickly behaved himself as he enjoyed the pats after the meditation from all the members. I sometimes gathered as many as 25 people in these meditation groups, especially when I invited a psychic reader near to Christmas, or when I invited spiritual authors who were promoting their books. I am hoping that I will be able to do the same when I come to the marketing and promotion of this book!! What a wonderful feeling that will be!

The voluntary networking, the workshops I have run, and the many positions in which I've been employed have all helped me to find the path to my success, in my passion for

Spiritual growth 43-57 years

the life path I am here to attain.

As time goes on I feel I have had a wealth of knowledge, and different scenarios in my life to help me with my journey. I may have missed out some of the situations, but I feel I have mentioned the most important ones that anyone who reads this book will be able to relate to, and perhaps glean information which will enable them to start their own journey to spiritual enlightenment.

In 2007 I decided to become a Reiki Master and found a lady called Irene, north of the river, to teach me my Mastership. This I feel was the icing on the cake, as I was then able to teach people to do Reiki 1 and then Reiki II, and then if need be become a Master themselves. I felt after this that I had really come into my own passion and enjoyment of life. I seem to have found where I was in my life and was now able to enjoy the serenity of things – such simple things gave me so much enjoyment.

In February that year, around the time of our anniversary on February 17, we embarked on our first cruise, on the Gemini cruise ship. This we boarded at Singapore then sailed up the Malacca Straits for seven days, which was a beautiful experience – stopping at Kuala Lumpur, Langkawi, Krabi Island, Phuket, and Penang before heading back to

The Journey to my Life Purpose

Singapore. During this cruise I wrote in my journal. I also wrote a talk for my meditation group on Reiki healing, its history, benefits and how it can help if you need energy or stress relief in your life. I found this talk started my journey into teaching others my passion, and integrating this passion into my daily life by helping others. This I felt was my life purpose.

When I returned home to Perth I began clearing away many other things from my life in order to enhance my journey. I started to do monthly meditation workshops from my house in Bicton. At that point I started teaching Reiki 1, 2 and Reiki Masters (Level 3) workshops, and moved my practice from Melville House to my own home Bicton.

During April 2007 I managed to find a client and friend to set up a website for my healing business, which I named "The Healing Experience". I came across this name when I was walking my dog Oliver. In fact, when I came to think about it, I seemed to have a lot of ideas and inspirations about my life and business in spirituality whilst I walked my beautiful dog Oliver. I also found I did many of my meditations when I walked him, and we both sat and looked over the river at Bicton near the quarantine park.

In the previous year, 2006, at the Everywoman Expo, I'd

Spiritual growth 43-57 years

managed to find a lady who did business coaching sessions. She offered to give me sessions in exchange for healing and massage or reflexology. She gave me tremendous encouragement and made me feel very good about myself, and this positivity helped me get my life on track. Eventually this lady moved to Melbourne with the business, and I felt she seemed much more settled there in the cooler climate.

In May 2007 I had to travel to the UK to help my mum and dad get over illnesses. I went there to cheer them on. Mum was getting over shingles and Dad was recovering from glaucoma. They were both quite depressed so I helped them look forward to life again and I was happy that I could be there for them. My Reiki was surely a great asset at this time and I thanked God for giving me these skills!!

By July 2007 I was gradually forming a very good support network around me, and I was building my clientele, while at the same time doing workshops, business networking and professional women's events. My personal health support person was a naturopath who came to my house once a month to assess me and give me iridology – which is checking the eyes for any ill health or nutritional deficiencies. I had a mentor to help keep me on track with my business. I did water aerobics three times a week to keep supple and energised. Another great support was my dog

The Journey to my Life Purpose

Oliver, who helped me with walking and meditation.

In September 2007 I started some healing work in a spiritual shop in Fremantle – this only lasted a few weeks, as healing does not seem to be a modality that suits a shop situation. The shop was more a psychic reading place. I felt I learnt a lot from doing this exercise, as it taught me that healing needs to be done in a calm and safe environment.

On 26 November 2007 I decided to do some voluntary work for the King Edward Hospital in Subiaco. I started working in the dietitians' office as assistant secretary of that department. This was my way of giving back to the community and I enjoyed this interaction with the staff very much. I was provided with free parking and a free lunch. I looked at doing another session of volunteer work at King Edward Hospital, and found this led to part-time secretarial work in the Genetics Department in October 2008.

During 2008 I was very busy with my healing business and also had a trip away to join my husband, who was working hard in Wollongong near Sydney. I met up with some wonderful business people and saw how life was on the east coast of Australia – a very enjoyable experience. Some of the highlights of that trip were:

Spiritual growth 43-57 years

1. A visit to the biggest Buddhist temple in the southern hemisphere.
2. An International Women's Day event at the Novatel Langley hotel in Wollongong, where I won an Easter raffle prize of a basket of chocolate and wine.
3. Joining a meditation group and water aerobics class in Wollongong.
4. Visiting a Reiki Master and enjoying an interaction with her.
5. Meeting some wonderful people who made my stay in Wollongong very worthwhile.

In 2010 I decided to add another string to my bow and become a psychic reader, doing numerology, photo readings, Angel readings and spiritual medium work. I am still doing this and participate in psychic fairs in Perth or surrounding areas. I also do psychic dinners and parties for groups of people from time to time. As I draw into retirement I still feel I will be able to do this, but on a word-of-mouth basis.

The Journey to my Life Purpose

- CHAPTER 5 -

Overcoming Problems 57 -59 years

My daughter

When I started my journalling in May 2005, I was going through a difficult period of my life, dealing with my daughter (my eldest twin of 24 years) who was going through anorexia, anxiety and depression. She seemed at times beyond help and it was an uphill struggle to keep her motivated and positive, and to obtain the right sort of help. We tried several avenues of help through the medical

The Journey to my Life Purpose

profession, to no avail. I was told to write a journal of my feelings to help me to come to terms with her illness, and to also help me deal with this situation. By writing my frustrations down on paper I was able to step back from the ongoing trauma and see things a little more clearly. I was then in a better position to make a decision about the best course of help for her. I understand that my daughter went through many bad emotions/feelings at this time, and couldn't sleep most of the time at night but slept all day. I became extremely frustrated and angry at her and the only thing I could do was turn to my journalling. She always had to come to shopping with me so that I wouldn't get her anything that would make her fat!!

On 6 May 2005 she tried to take her life for the second time, and luckily we got to hospital just in time. My eldest daughter, who is a Social Worker at the local hospital, had heard about an organisation called "Teen Challenge". They help young people to face up to their problems through Christian ethos. We made inquiries with "Teen Challenge" and managed to obtain an interview for her to chat with the administrator in the office in Perth. We did make progress little by little with her, and I think this interview, which addressed "Teen Challenge" started to help her with answers to coping with life.

Overcoming problems 57-59 years

The appointment with Teen Challenge in Kingsley took place on 11 May 2005. This seemed like a step in the right direction for my daughter, and she seemed willing to go along and hear what they had to say. I felt spirit helped with this in order to free me to do my own healing work, which I knew was in my heart. My daughter saw a lady called Avis, who explained the ups and downs of life in Teen Challenge at Esperance. There would be many challenges for her, but I was sure it would be the making of her in the long run. Teen Challenge has a Christian ethos, but I felt that would help her to grow – after all we had I hope taught her the rights and wrongs of life, and she would still hang on to them!! This was a great challenge for me also, to step back and let her go, and find out for herself. It would take approximately two years for her to come out of this, so I hoped spirit would help her along the right path for her sake!! You will hear later on in this book how things materialised.

On 30 May 2005 I took my daughter for another appointment at Teen Challenge in Perth to talk to one of the girls who had just completed the challenge. Asking questions about it would hopefully give her the confidence to make her mind up about this transformation in her life. My daughter took high doses of Valium, so we had to see if they would accept her, and wean her off them.

The Journey to my Life Purpose

On 15 June 2005 I took my daughter for her final interview for Teen Challenge, and she was accepted. She flew down to Esperance on June 23rd 2005, which was a Thursday. She was very teary and upset at the news, but realised that we had tried to get her better through doctors and specialists, and it hadn't worked! Teen Challenge would, and I felt the angels would help her to make it happen for herself!! We said goodbye to her at the airport, and she was picked up by Teen Challenge in Esperance. This was another challenge for me, and it helped me to let go of my daughter, to allow her to live her own life in her own way. We were not permitted to contact her for 14 days, as this was a period of adjustment for her! My husband was also going away on business, so I had more adjustments to make. I would learn to be positive with this break, and also ask the angels to send me guidance at this time!

Initially I felt rather lost dealing with my feelings on my own – but I think these times happen for a reason, and help you to come to terms with what you have gone through, and how to move on in your life.

My lovely friends helped me move on in my life. They came together to give me support and they took me out to different events in Perth. I was also busy with my grandson Ethan and his first birthday celebrations, so these and other

Overcoming problems 57-59 years

things were of help with my situation.

We all managed to speak to my daughter on the phone for the first time since she went to Esperance on Thursday, 14 July 2005, and she seemed much more positive in her voice. Our first visit to see her in Esperance was scheduled for August 2005.

By mid July 2005 my healing business was starting to take off with more clients booking in the Melville Centre. This made me realise that once my stress levels had declined, spirit sent me more people to be helped through my healing massage etc. This was another challenge for me at this time, and I felt spirit also would not give me too many clients, as I had not yet sorted out this big problem with my daughter and my relationship with my husband.

I do think my journey to spiritual enlightenment was meant to have all these ups and downs during this stage. It allowed me to progress into the wonderful joys and excitement which would happen ahead.

At the end of June 2005 I met a lady called Trish who was at the Everywoman Expo in Perth, and she had a stand with her coaching business named "Harmony Wellness". She offered me a free coaching session and also wanted to speak

The Journey to my Life Purpose

to me about a course in self-development, which would put me on the right track with my career.

On the 21 of July 2005 I had my first counselling and coaching session with Trish, and found her advice encouraging and uplifting. She also taught me to look at the pitfalls in life in a positive and encouraging way. In fact she encouraged me to turn all negative aspects of my life into positive ones. I also managed to arrange to work with Trish in exchange for my healing sessions, which I felt was a very good arrangement.

I found that once I met Trish and started these coaching sessions other parts of my life seemed to be turning around. Firstly, my relationship with my husband was better. He asked me to help him move to a new office to start a new job as a drafting coordinator, which was a promotion for him. Secondly, my business seem to be on the upward trend in the Melville house and Rikki (the owner of the room) was happy to support me in this by giving me more days there. Thirdly, my daughter was progressing very well at Teen Challenge, and had made some new friends. She seemed to have some wonderful positive influences around her, and I thanked God and the angels for answering my prayers, and helping me to sort her life out! Other things that were good in my life were my wonderful grandson Ethan, who I love with all my heart and who did and does give me great

Overcoming problems 57-59 years

joy! I am grateful for his unconditional love. I was grateful to former girlfriends, all of whom gave me support in my life, and my other daughters who were there for me when necessary.

Around this time I visited Becky, the clairvoyant and counsellor, who told me that my daughter would reach a crossing point in life in five months – October/November 2005.

At the beginning of August 2005 I found that Ricki, the owner of the room I rent in Melville House, began to take an active interest in me, wanting to be my mentor in a business sense. This was another step in a good direction for my spirituality.

On the 6 August 2005 we drove to Esperance from Bicton to visit my daughter at Teen Challenge. Her attitude was much more positive and we were both very pleased with what she had achieved in six weeks. The journey down there was very long, 750 km; we set off at 6 am and arrived at 4:30 pm. Our daughter was very pleased we were there to visit, and the people who ran the Teen Challenge seemed very supportive to her. However she still had a lot of work to do in order to feel happier in herself. I do feel spirit answered my prayers about her condition of anorexia and drug abuse,

The Journey to my Life Purpose

and I felt my daughter had been given a second chance with life. I knew I was little bit concerned about religious indoctrination, but considering where my daughter had been in her life, if a religious program could help her then that's all that mattered. The Teen Challenge workers were another set of people who've brought meaning to me, by helping these teenagers who were caught up with drug abuse etc.

On Thursday, 18 August 2005 I meet with the Small Business Association to see a specialist marketing advisor in the Perth office. He gave me some ideas on how to market my business so that I could report back to my coaching partner Trish. Also he suggested advertising more with cards, brochures and email/Internet. I must admit I wasn't too keen about that advice, but at least I didn't have to outlay any cash for their services.

My eldest daughter had supported me through my journey of spirituality, but little did I know that she and her boyfriend, Sean, had ended their relationship of 11 years. She moved into our house on Saturday 3rd of September 2005. The house was full again – I didn't know if I would be able to run a business from there; I would possibly have to look at running the business solely from Melville house or look for other premises. My other daughter was also

Overcoming problems 57-59 years

coming home – she'd had an accident at "Teen Challenge" and broken her coccyx, and they couldn't look after her down there. She had to sleep with her eldest sister as I had run out of beds!!

Rikki, my business mentor in Melville House, had agreed to give me more days to see my clients, so I was now doing Mondays, Thursdays and Saturdays, and was now able to move out of my house and concentrate on running the business from Melville house – which made a lot of sense!! My business needed to be away from home at that time – there were too many scenarios with the family going on, and it was not conducive to the wellness of my clientele.

Towards the end of September 2005 my daughter returned to Esperance and things settled down at home. Business at Melville house started to take off with plenty of clients – basically through word-of-mouth. Suddenly I felt things were starting to turn around for me. I so loved doing my healing; it made me feel special again inside, in fact it made me feel that I could conquer anything on my own!

In October 2005 I realised that my friend Lynn (whom I met through working at Child and Adolescent Mental Health Services) has been quite supportive in my spiritual journey. She's quite spiritual herself and likes to accompany

The Journey to my Life Purpose

me to Expos and spiritual events that seem to interest her.

On Sunday, October 9, 2005 Lynn and I went to see Doreen Virtue at an event in Burswood. We both bought a few of her things, like cards and CDs, and had a good day listening to her talks and readings and spiritual affirmations. A good day was had by both of us!!

At this stage I was finding life was still pretty hectic, with running a business part-time, running a house part-time, and being all things to all people in my family. I did feel I had a good network of friends who gave me support, and would listen to me to help me through the pitfalls that seem to come up. Life I feel is very much like that, but as my confidence grew and I learned to trust my judgement about what steps to take next on my spiritual journey, I found my support network just seemed to be there for me.

I am pleased to say that at the time of writing this book, my daughter – after all the ups and downs her illness – managed to come out of "Teen Challenge" in 2007. When she graduated my husband and I were invited to a special ceremony in Esperance, and the difference in her whole attitude to life was amazing, and we both had tears of joy at her outcome. It took great courage on her part to relate bad experiences before going into "Teen Challenge", and I

Overcoming problems 57-59 years

can honestly say it takes guts to come out of there with a turnaround to the positive experience of life. She still has her ups and downs now, but she has the skills now and a wonderful partner to help her overcome them.

She has now completed her four year state registered nurse degree and postgraduate studies. She's a wonderful nurse and we as parents are very proud of her. For all those parents and teenagers who are experiencing the traumas of "anorexia", please hang in there and believe in you, and also ask spirit or the angels to help you get through – it works – believe me I know from experience!!

My Marriage

My husband and I have been married for 42 years (as of 2015) and I can honestly say it has been a very happy marriage, but as in all marriages, there are times when you feel you are drifting apart, and these times can be quite stressful and upsetting. Before arriving in Australia, I went through a very difficult period after having my twin daughters, and I experienced postnatal depression. I mentioned this earlier on in my journey. This period was quite fraught with bringing up three small children under five, financial difficulties, having no support nearby and

The Journey to my Life Purpose

generally working long hours to keep our "heads above water" so to speak. At this time, when I was crying most of the time, my husband took to drinking – of course, it was his way of dealing with things!! I guess we were both quite young and didn't know how to deal with emotions very well! In other words we had to learn to communicate with each other a lot better. We had become so busy, we didn't have time for each other. This went on for some time until I fell apart, and we had to have some counselling to address the problem.

When we came to Australia we had a new life and new opportunities so we became much closer learning about all the new ways of living here. Also Australia was a much more positive country and the weather made all the difference to our lifestyle.

My husband was pursuing different interests to me. I was looking at all aspects of my interest in spirituality as well as setting up a business within a room in Melville House, Canning Highway and looking at other premises in a centre for healing where workshops are held. My three girls were still acknowledging me for Mother's Day and taking me out for lunch and spoiling me, which gave me a good feeling!

On the 31 of May 2005 I wrote in my journal of the meeting

Overcoming problems 57-59 years

I had with Becky, the clairvoyant and counsellor who was helping me with my relationship as well as with my daughter. I wrote: "My relationship needs to be nurtured and I need to give him 10 minutes each night when he comes home from work to communicate about the day and give him positive strokes".

It is interesting in my journalling at this stage of my life (May 2005) that I felt unwanted by my husband – obviously then I didn't have the awareness I do now to overcome problems and work them out properly. I also felt my spirituality was becoming hard for my husband to understand, and he was unable to share my passion as he didn't believe in it, but I did recognise that he still loved me in spite of that!

My daughter's problems needed to be addressed, as my husband and myself were growing apart, and I didn't want this to happen, because I felt we were meant to be together, and share the ups and downs of life. He is my rock and grounds me so that I can do this wonderful spiritual work which is a yearning in my heart.

On Thursday, 7 July 2005 my husband returned home from his working trip in Kalgoorlie and I was pleased to see him. We booked a night at the Duxton Hotel, Perth on the Saturday, and a special dinner at the revolving

The Journey to my Life Purpose

restaurant on the 33rd floor of St Martin's Tower in Perth. There was a beautiful view of Perth that night. My husband needed some relaxing time before he started work again on Monday. Our relationship seemed to be getting back on track – but I had to admit life was very much up and down, so having my own spiritual beliefs helped me to put things into perspective again.

At this time in my life my husband and I seem to be doing social things apart from each other and this was positive in a way; we both grew separately, and this allowed us to come together again. I have learned quite a bit from marriage, and it seems that couples who go through these ups and downs experience a certain flow, as shown in the diagram opposite:

Overcoming problems 57-59 years

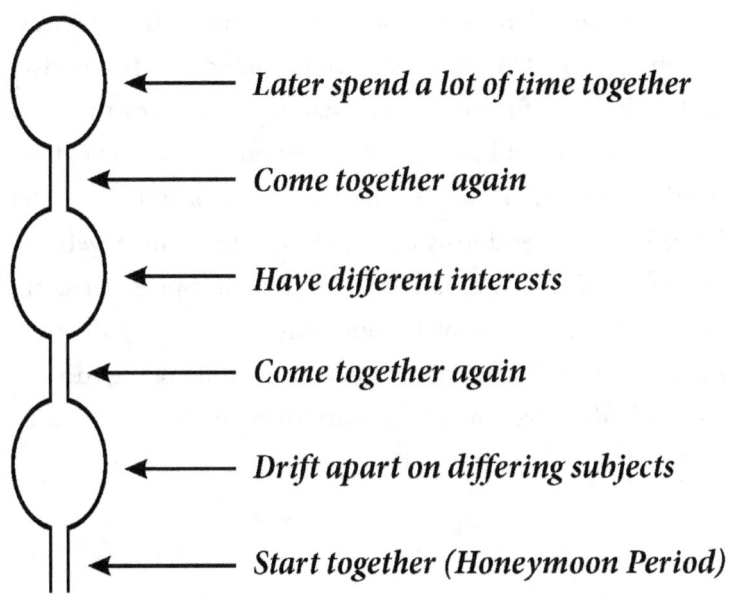

In my early 50s I worked as a medical secretary for a number of years around the public hospitals in Perth – this gave me a lot of experience. Also at this time I decided to set up a small business in healing, massage and reflexology. I decided to work part-time in both these fields in order to fund the set up of my business.

At the end of 2004 I decided, with the help of spirit, to leave my position at Fremantle Hospital and take on my business

The Journey to my Life Purpose

full-time. This took a while to really take off, as I had family problems, and I needed finances to market the business. Eventually, in 2006, things started to materialise fund-wise, with help from the position I'd had as a secretary in BP in London. Little did I know that a pension was being held for me there, and after making enquiries it was sent to me. This helped me tremendously and I was able to set up a website, do some advertising, and market myself. Spirit certainly helped me to trust that I would have the money there to fund my business, but of course we as human beings do not always believe we can wholeheartedly trust in this for it to materialize.

- CHAPTER 6 -

Enjoying later life

In 2008 I decided to move in a new direction and become a Marriage Celebrant. I was still going to keep my healing business going, but I felt I wanted to follow this new passion. This I had to learn over four days (two weekends) with a teacher who had also been a Civil Marriage Celebrant for a number of years.

I knew marriage celebrancy was a completely new direction for me, but felt it was the right choice and the right time for

The Journey to my Life Purpose

me to do it.

While I also knew it was a completely different role to my other passion, I still felt I could manage both businesses.

At this time, April 2015, I have made the decision to retire from my marriage celebrancy business. I have enjoyed the seven years that I have worked in the industry but I have now lost the passion. Things are changing in the world as regards to marriage. Most young people do not want to commit to a partner, and this is what marriage is about. So I feel I have done my time as a Marriage Celebrant, and I feel I have had the best years with this passion.

In recent years, since July 2010, we moved from Bicton into a lifestyle village in Baldivis. This we decided to do, as we felt we wanted to downsize from our house in Bicton, and also free ourselves up for travelling overseas and doing some caravanning around Australia. At the time we moved into our house in Baldivis, my husband was still working long hours in Perth, and I was working two businesses part-time. Before we moved, I started a one day per week position doing psychic readings in a spiritual shop in Rockingham, and this helped me to meet people before I moved into the area. I also found a community centre in Wellard, near Kwinana, where I could do my healings and also attract

Enjoying later life

clients, especially on the pampering days that were held periodically. I felt I was becoming very independent and self-sufficient in my own right, but I was also in a safe community. This safe community was something that I enjoyed at this point in time, as my husband was going overseas quite a lot with his work, and I felt very safe with the security gate on the village at night. The people were also very friendly and helpful, and I felt I could see people in the village without getting too familiar with them. My life was a joy and I felt very contented with my lot in life. I missed my husband when he went on long trips, but I felt I could hold my own as a female without having to ask for help.

In October 2010 I managed to secure another position as a psychic reader in a bookshop in Como, Perth and enjoyed this very much until the travelling up and down the freeway became a bit exhausting.

In the latter part of 2010 my eldest daughter took long service leave from her Senior Social Work position at Royal Perth Hospital, and decided to go and live in London to experience a busy life. She certainly had that, and found the pace somewhat different, but enjoyed the challenge. She took her partner with her, and in August 2011 they decided to get married on a boat on the River Thames.

The Journey to my Life Purpose

That same year my dear dad died in February, and I went to England in April/May to help my mum with her grief and my own. This was a very trying and emotional time for me, and my mum. I am grateful to have this country Australia to come home to, as it brings me such a lot of positivity, and helps me to cope with the grief of my dad's passing. I was very grateful that I had my healings, readings and weddings – this makes me feel I am helping others in my life. I talked to my mum regularly on the phone each week and helped her to stay positive, but she didn't seem to lift herself. I guess when you have been married for 67 years it is hard to continue life alone. Her birthday was coming up, so I decided to go and visit her for the special day when she turned 90. We had some good times whilst I was there, and we took some coach trips to Sheringham in Norfolk. Also we visited Bournemouth in Hants and we enjoyed each other's company. I was pleased when I left that she seemed much like her 'old self".

When I returned to Australia, my husband decided to take me in the caravan to Coral Bay, a special place in north-west of Australia. This place has just one road in and out, and when you go for a paddle in the ocean the fish (which are called "Red Emperor") swim between your legs when you feed them. You feel as though "you have died and gone to heaven!" It's a very relaxing place and is always there

Enjoying later life

when you need it!! The only negative thing about it is that it takes about 2 to 3 days to drive there!!!

In September 2012 my husband was out of work and did not feel he was ready for retirement. He decided to set up a small business while trying to find work, but the work didn't seem to materialise. We celebrated our Ruby Wedding Anniversary in February 2013, and decided to go on a cruise around the top end of Australia. This helped us to have a nice well-earned break and we enjoyed this very much. In August 2013 my husband managed to secure more design work in Perth and stayed until February 2014.

In March 2014 my dearest mum died and my sisters and I were unable to get there in time, but my brother was by her side. I managed to fly over for the funeral and my husband and myself went back again in June 2014. We had already planned this holiday, little knowing that my mum was going to pass away.

In May 2014 we took a long trip to Canada and the UK for a total of four months. We enjoyed our first three weeks in Toronto, Canada visiting my husband's brother and family. While there we visited a few sights, including Niagara Falls and the sixth tallest skyscraper building in the world. It was quite cold for May but gradually improved the week we

The Journey to my Life Purpose

were leaving.

In June 2014 we flew into Southend airport in the UK, to be met by my son-in-law who is married to my eldest daughter. They have just recently had our third grandchild, a little girl called Darcey. She is so beautiful and so small but a joy to behold!! We stayed in the UK for three months and visited family and friends. We also travelled 4000 miles whilst we were there, visiting Scotland, the Lake District, Yorkshire, Shropshire, Essex and a few other places. We returned home to Australia at the end of August 2014 and felt absolutely exhausted. After a few days we decided to take the caravan to Coral Bay to "veg out" as Australians say.

It is now April 2015 and I am looking forward to travelling yet again. We are off to Crete in Greece for three weeks at the end of May.

Then we will be having two weeks at home, and after that we set off on our journey to Queensland in north east of Australia.

My life is a very pleasant experience at this point in time, and I guess it should be – after all when you are retired you are supposed to enjoy it, and that is what we intend to do,

Enjoying later life

as long as we are fit and healthy! I hope all of you who reach this point in your life, and can enjoy this experience to the full too!!

The Journey to my Life Purpose

- CHAPTER 7 -

My personal history

Starting from when I was born, I worked through my timeline and listed each year of progress until the present day.

I started this journal of my life in 2005, when I was 55. For each of my 55 years I noted down the special events that I remembered; obviously events occurring before I was five were not very significant to me, as I was unable to clearly remember this time of my life, and could not ask my mum,

The Journey to my Life Purpose

who lived in the UK. I also felt it was more important to list what seemed relevant to me rather than my mum.

My Timeline

BIRTH TO 2 YEARS ~ I was born on the first day of June 1949, and I am the second child of four. I have a brother who is four years older and two sisters. One sister is two years younger and the other is four years younger than me. I have no personal recollection of what happened during this period of my life.

3 YEARS ~ I remember living in a bungalow, which is a single storey house. My Aunty Wendy came to visit us quite regularly, and she was a policewoman. The sight of her uniform always frightened me at this age.

4 YEARS ~ used to walk to the local shops for a loaf of bread for my mum, thought it was a very long way from my house – I went back on a visit years later and it was only a few steps away. We moved house to the north of England from the south. My dad starts a new job as a primary school teacher. I wasn't impressed with my new surroundings.

5 YEARS ~ I start school – going with my dad on the bus as

My personal history

we didn't have a car in those days. I have trouble with the zip on my raincoat on the first day!

6 YEARS ~ I don't like school very much – find it hard to make friends. My dad is a teacher at the same school. Had pneumonia, spent several weeks in hospital.

7 YEARS ~ I still find it hard to settle – have made a few friends. The girl next door to me, called Freda, is a bit of a show off and a bully.

8 YEARS ~ Dad gets a promotion to a new school. My teacher doesn't like this and tries to victimise me in class. Mum and Dad move me and my younger sister to a new school called Riddlesden Primary School, which is much better, and I make some good friends.

9 YEARS ~ I achieve first prize for handwriting in a competition run by Brooke Bond Tea for the whole of UK schools – and win a Cookery Book worth seven shillings and sixpence.

10 TO 11 YEARS ~ I sit my 11+ examinations (these determine which kind of high school you will attend). At this age I learnt Scottish country dancing which I enjoyed very much. Dad moves on to new position as Headmaster

The Journey to my Life Purpose

at a Primary School in Hebden Bridge – so we move house. Start new school where Dad is Headmaster – don't like it.

12 YEARS ~ I start senior school – Calder High Comprehensive – don't really like it but begin to make new friends.

13 YEARS ~ We live at the Vicarage in a place called Mytholmroyd. The reason we are there, is we are unable to find a house. The Vicar is on the Council and we apply for rented accommodation. There are no rented houses available, so he invites us to live with him. We end up staying there for four years.

14 YEARS ~ I become involved in church activities such as choir and amateur dramatics.

15 YEARS ~ I become a Beatles fan. We leave Yorkshire in the north of England for Hertfordshire in the south. I start another school for the last year of school – hate being there as it's so hard to make friends, and I find it very difficult to catch up – the result being that I fail my exams!

16 YEARS ~ I decide to find myself a job and start work with the local council as a Junior Clerk. I earn £24 per month and give Mum my keep. I also go to Day Release at

My personal history

Ware College to learn typing etc.

17 YEARS ~ I'm still working and socialising with friends.

18 YEARS ~ I joined 18+ for social activities. I also changed jobs and work in a hospital as Medical Records Clerk – I didn't enjoy this, so after three months I leave, and go back to the County Council in the Children's Department. I work as an Audio Secretary for one year and also with a small electrical company.

19 YEARS ~ I meet Robin – serious boyfriend – first love. I start a new job in London with British Petroleum, the best secretarial job ever!!

20 YEARS ~ I pass my driving test. Meet boyfriend Mick who is a butcher – he was second serious love – we get engaged. I go to Jersey for my first holiday with a girlfriend.

21 YEARS ~ I'm still working at BP. I break off engagement to Mick, after realising he was very different to me. I go to Spain for holiday with a girlfriend.

22 YEARS ~ I go to Yugoslavia with my friend Ruth – didn't really enjoy this holiday, not very good weather. At work I move to Human Resources and love it – best job I ever had!

The Journey to my Life Purpose

November 1971 – I meet my husband, the love of my life. I go on holidays to Greece with my friend Linda – lovely place. When I come home I decide to get engaged to my husband (July 1972).

23 YEARS ~ I move job to Harlow BP – wrong move – didn't like it! My grandma dies in 1972, the year before my wedding. On February 17, 1973 my husband and I marry (and have been married now for 42 years). The first house we lived in was a one-bedroom flat with oak beams, and we are very happy there together. We meet some special friends during our year in the flat.

24 YEARS ~ We move to another flat in Harlow to save money for a house – it takes a year to save the deposit. We saw Elton John at Watford Football Club (my husband had me on his shoulders watching the show – wouldn't happen now!!) On December 31, 1974 my dear Uncle John, my mother's twin brother, dies.

25 YEARS ~ We move to our own house at Newport Essex – it is lovely and beautiful and I am feeling very happy! I move to a much better job with BP in London.

26 YEARS ~ still enjoying job at BP in London and commuting from Newport to London. We go to the Isle of

My personal history

Wight for a holiday with great friends – we do this for two years running.

27 YEARS ~ I move job again in BP, this time working with lovely people in Human Resources – but the job is quite stressful. I am expecting our first child and I have problems during the first three months, so move to a less stressful position until I leave after 8 years service.

28 YEARS ~ Louise Helen is born – our first child – 7 lbs 15 oz – breach birth – ouch!! Lovely baby, very good.

29 YEARS ~ I enjoy being mum to Louise. She is christened at three months in Newport Church. My younger sister and her husband come from Australia to visit.

30 YEARS ~ I don't like being 30 and feel quite old. We move to Milton Keynes and I become pregnant. We were told at five months we were expecting twins.

31 YEARS ~ Twins born, both girls – Amy 6 lbs 11 oz, Julia 6 lbs 6 oz. Lovely babies but hard work with Louise a toddler of three years.

32 YEARS ~ The twins are 10 months old and I suffer severe depression – can't cope so go to Mum's for a few days for

The Journey to my Life Purpose

rest. I have a support system put in place by the Health Visitor: Nurse, Social Worker and Student Child Nurse come to help. What a relief!!

33 YEARS ~ I experience the early stages of menopause. We take a holiday in Bournemouth with girls – a lovely time – weather gorgeous.

34 YEARS ~ The girls are growing up and I start a new job, just a few hours per week to keep my brain ticking over. It is working with teachers of English as a Second Language. We go on holiday to Bournemouth again.

35 YEARS ~ I'm still doing the job at English as a Second Language, though I only work school term. My sister comes from Australia for a holiday and this gives us an idea to emigrate.

36 YEARS ~ Our application for Australian residency is granted.

37 YEARS ~ We arrive in Western Australia on the 4th January 1987. We are a little perplexed with life here. The girls enjoy school. We stay with my sister and her husband for six weeks. We move into our own house 14th of February 1987 and my husband gets a job on the 9th of February

My personal history

1987. I take a little longer – July 1987.

38 YEARS ~ Australia is good to us. We are all settled residents and I start to work at Boans as a Shop Assistant.

39 YEARS ~ I find work part-time mornings 8 to 12 as a receptionist at a car yard.

40 YEARS ~ My husband and I celebrate our 40th birthdays with friends and family at the Chalet Healy in Perth hills. We all enjoy a 60s dress up night with a meal and transport in a London bus.

41 YEARS ~ My older brother and family come for a holiday. We are enjoying life with house and new swimming pool. My husband is working away all week, which causes a bit of friction in our marriage – he is missing out on the girl's development.

42 YEARS ~ My husband has a 21 again party. Our friends Dave and Jeanette get married.

43 YEARS ~ I start work at a new job – Fremantle Cemetery Board. I enjoy the new job very much; it brings variety, including giving people grief counselling both on phone and face-to-face. I worked at the Cemetery for three years

The Journey to my Life Purpose

and gain a lot of experience. Because of this I become aware of spirituality!!!

44 YEARS ~ Life is good at present, I am enjoying my job and social life.

45 YEARS ~ My dear friends from the UK visit us for a holiday. I also visit the UK for the first time in seven years for Mum and Dad's Golden Wedding Anniversary.

46 YEARS ~ For Christmas 1995 we enjoy a holiday at Denmark, WA with friends – best Christmas ever!!

47 YEARS ~ We move to Bicton to a new house – good move! Our eldest daughter moves out of family home to live with her boyfriend. We join the local Yacht Club.

48 YEARS ~ We buy a boat with my sister and her husband. I leave my job at the Cemetery to work as a Medical Secretary in Public Hospitals contracting.

49/50 YEARS ~ I enjoy living at Bicton and enjoy the social life at the Yacht Club.

51 YEARS ~ I go to the UK for a holiday with two of my girls.

My personal history

52 YEARS ~ I work as a Medical Secretary for a number of years around the public hospitals in Perth – this gives me a lot of experience. I also go to the UK for Mum and Dad's Diamond Wedding Anniversary in 1994.

53 YEARS ~ I started working part-time in a new business doing Reiki healing and massage/reflexology, whilst still doing Medical Secretarial work.

56 YEARS ~ I leave hospital work and decide to do business full time. I go into some shared rooms in Melville House near home and progress from strength to strength.

57 YEARS ~ I start running Meditation Groups from my house in Bicton on the last Sunday afternoon of the month. I find reputable speakers to come along and talk about their businesses. Sometimes as many as 22 people attend these workshops – very successful!

58 YEARS ~ I am coping with my middle daughter's struggle with anorexia (this has been going on for two years) – she eventually goes to Teen Challenge in Esperance for rehabilitation work. She comes out successful and recovers to a more fulfilling life training as a nurse.

59 YEARS ~ I visit Wollongong, New South Wales with my

The Journey to my Life Purpose

husband for a month. We enjoy the break – my husband worked and the company flew me over to be with him. In September this year I become a Civil Marriage Celebrant after studying, and placing an application with the Attorney Generals Department.

60 YEARS ~ In January of this year David, my husband's brother, comes to Australia for a holiday and we take him to Kalbarri. In March 2009 my youngest daughter married Joel in Nannup, Western Australia, and I officiated at the wedding as a Celebrant (my first wedding). My husband celebrated his 60th birthday at the yacht club, and I had my birthday celebration in Bali at Sanur and Lembongan Island.

61 YEARS ~ I have a few weddings to officiate at this year and also find my home-based healing business takes off. This year we move again from Bicton to a lifestyle village in Baldivis. We have a month before we can move into our home, so we live with friends and my sister and her husband for a few weeks. We move into our house on 9th of July 2010. In the October of this year I work in Como, Perth as a Psychic Reader and enjoy this very much until the travelling up and down the freeway becomes a bit exhausting.

My personal history

62 YEARS ~ This year my eldest daughter is in the UK after being granted a one year long service leave from Royal Perth Hospital. While there she marries her partner Matt on August 20, 2011 on a boat on the River Thames. I don't officiate at this wedding!! My eldest daughter and Matt return to Australia in October 2011 to their place in Bicton.

63 YEARS ~ My dear Dad dies in February and I go to be with Mum to help with her grief and my own in April/May 2011. My husband is still working. I am still busy with weddings and healings. I also go to the UK for Mum's 90th birthday, and then my husband and I go to Coral Bay for 21 days – lovely!! My daughter and Matt return to the UK to live and buy a house.

64 YEARS ~ My husband is off work from September 2012 until August 2013 and isn't ready for retirement. He tries to work for himself in a small business but that doesn't help. He eventually goes back to design work in Perth and stays until February 2014. I am still doing healings and weddings.

65 YEARS ~ This year has been very busy travelling. My husband and I are both in our 65th year and we enjoy a three week holiday in Canada for three weeks with Peter's brother. . We also travel around the UK visiting family and friends. My husband is now retired and seems to be

The Journey to my Life Purpose

accepting it. I am now writing this book with the goal of having it ready for publication in July 2015.

66 years ~ We are planning our overseas holiday to Crete, Greece for May 2015 until end of June 2015. In July 2015 we are planning our trip in the caravan to Queensland via South Australia – Coober Pedy – the Opal Mines, Uluru near Ayres Rock, and across to the Queensland coast. We plan to make our way down the east coast, and then along the bottom coast to home, arriving approximately November 2015. In December 2015 we are having our daughter and son-in-law from England with their daughter Darcey for a holiday here in Australia for two weeks to stay with us!

Part two

Tips for inner peace

The Journey to my Life Purpose

- CHAPTER 8 -

Keeping a journal

I started a Journal of events in my life on 4 May 2005 (this being, incidentally, my husband's birthday and my dad's). From keeping this journal I learnt a great deal about myself and how to deal with emotions and feelings in my life. Writing things down instead of getting angry meant I no longer wasted energy with negative emotions. I was supposed to write a least three or four pages a day, but it slowly came down to one A4 page as I progressed. After every two days I had to highlight words which would give me

The Journey to my Life Purpose

insights into my life and mood, while the actions I needed to take were highlighted in another colour to differentiate the two. For each day I would plot out a "Pie Graph", which would tell me how life was going. From the centre point of a circle each category had a line drawn away from it to an outer circle. The categories I chose were relationship, exercise, work, family, self and assertiveness. By reading the journals you can see where the different categories went to on the line and join them accordingly. For example:

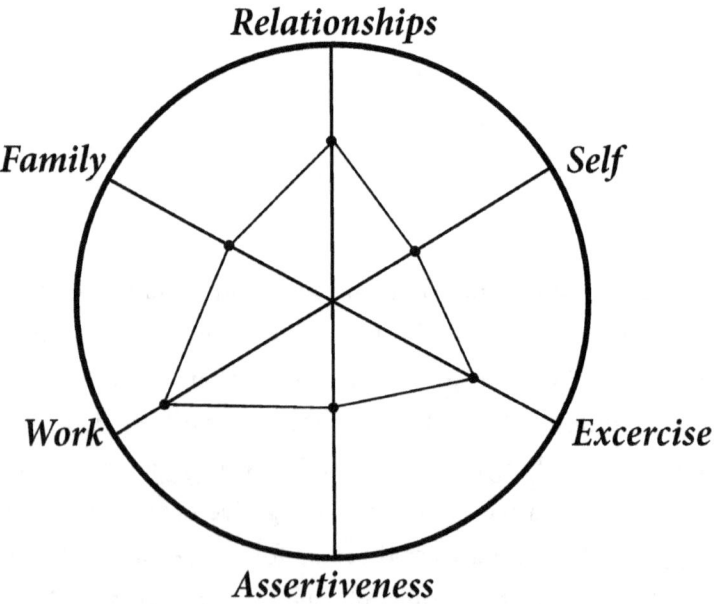

Keeping a journal

Each day, depending on what was written, you can put a mark on the line (which has a scale of 1 to 10) according to your perception of how you felt. This definitely helped me to assess where I was going in life, and showed me whether I was dealing with things positively or negatively. Writing things down certainly changed my way of thinking and helped me to get a different perspective on things in and around me.

As time progressed and I kept this journal going, I learnt to deal with things in my life a lot better. Writing them down and reflecting on them helped me to make better decisions in my life. I found that I was able to step back from arguments, and look at them from a different angle, and my thinking began to change.

I was also starting to see things around me. My favourite saying was "at last I can step back and smell the roses." I was learning my Reiki healing, and practising it, and I began to live, breathe and talk about this feeling to everyone who I felt would listen. However, I was careful not to indoctrinate people with my beliefs – those who I could see were not interested I left alone – if they were not interested I wasn't wasting my energy on them.

Through the journal writing I realised that the people you

The Journey to my Life Purpose

meet can make a difference in your progress with running a business – however big or small it is – sometimes make a difference to the goals you make, and how you learn to put them into action or, simply learn from them and don't follow them up!

Each day I wrote something down and sometimes it was not important. When it was important I could then refer back to that issue and either resolve it or take action on it accordingly. For example, in May 2006 I decided to take a job at a Montessori school in Cottesloe. The job was helping the school secretary for two days a week in school term time. This job was very good, but looking at my journal I noticed afterwards that I kept being ill whilst I was working there. This always seemed to come up for me in any job involving secretarial work, and it suddenly dawned on me that this work was not my passion and I loathed it. So in actual fact I needed to stop applying for this sort of work because it clearly was not for me.

A few days later, when I wrote this statement in my journal, I was told by spirit to resign from the position at the Montessori school and that the money would be in my bank account in the next few days. <u>What I had to do was trust the divine would help me.</u> In the next few days I went to draw money from a bank account and there was the

Keeping a journal

money – I nearly fainted – I trembled and couldn't believe it! My dreams had come true and I was self-sufficient and not dependent on anybody. It was a great feeling and I try to explain that to my clients when things are not going well for them, telling them to always put trust into their lives. I encourage them to write the affirmation "Money comes to me in abundance in perfect ways" twenty two times for 11 days, and then leave it and trust. It was certainly a big thing for me to gain the trust to put things into practice in my business and to do anything that I felt was worthwhile doing – like for instance writing this book for all those people who wish to start their spiritual journey, and feel stuck in their lives. It is not too late to follow your passion and go for it!

In the next few months, being October, November and December 2006, I decided to make a few purchases for myself – at last you may say!! I traded in my car, a Toyota Echo manual, for a Kia Rio automatic with all the bells and whistles on it. So on Tuesday, 10 October 2006 I picked a brand-new car with my daughter and baby Kaleb. Then on 12 October 2006 I booked a short holiday to Sydney with my friend Nancye – we went at the beginning of December, just before Christmas.

During October 2006 I had an influx of clients and a

The Journey to my Life Purpose

meditation workshop on the last Sunday of each month which had really taken off. This showed my business was really doing an about turn. Also I think my affirmations were bringing a lot of positivity into my life.

For journal writing I recommend "The Artists Way" by Julia Cameron. This book helped me with journal writing and showed me how to develop the "Pie Graph". It also helped me to deal with my feelings of anger, to be more sympathetic to others, and assess where I was going with my life purpose. There are many books to help you with journal writing; this one was recommended to me by a psychic/counsellor. I found that "The Artists Way" resonated with me, and I hope it helps you if you are interested in learning about journal writing, with a view to eventually becoming a writer.

- CHAPTER 9 -

Numerology

This modality I found very helpful, and I used it alongside my psychic clairvoyant readings. It has enhanced my connection with the client to obtain their birth date and eventually learn their life purpose number.

Another way of understanding your life purpose, or what you are here to achieve in this lifetime, is to learn Numerology. Numerology is a modality that has been going for hundreds of years!

The Journey to my Life Purpose

To find your life purpose number, add the numbers of your date of birth together and keep adding until you have a single digit. The exception to this is where the numbers add up to 11 or 22, in which case you don't reduce them further because these are master numbers.

For example, take my birth date:

1/6/1949

1 + **6** = 7 + **1** = 8 + **9** = 17 + **4** = 21 + **9** = 30/3 Numerology Number.

3 = My Life Path Number.

To find out what your number is for your current year (lets say it is 2015), put the day and month of your birth to 2015 and keep adding until you have a single figure number. For example using my birthdate:

1 + **6** = 7 + **2** = 9 + **1** = 10 + **5** = 15 : **1** + **5** = 6 – Number 6 would be my number this year.

Your year number starts manifesting two months before your birthday – mine would manifest on 1/4/2015.

Numerology

I will tell you a little bit about what each number says about you: –

1. This is a powerful number, implying a very singular person, who doesn't need others necessarily but enjoys a partner. Ones are often heads of organisations and people look to them for recognition and want to be like them. When you are in a number one year it's all about new beginnings for you – but you will also feel it is one step forward and three back, which can be quite frustrating!!
2. The number two person is inclined to "sit on the fence" in any complex or ordinary situation in life. Twos are very mellow people and do not like arguments! They tend to go along with the flow of anything that is going on. If you are in a two year it can be quite boring, as nothing seems to happen, if you have made any step forward in the previous year (Number 1) you must manifest it in year two, or else you will have the same old routine as you had before!
3. A number three person is very shy in their early years, and finds it very hard to interact with people. That all changes as they grow up – they become very socially active and it's a job to stop them from talking. This is because they tend to live on their nerves. They are very giving people, to their detriment, and also live a lot in self-doubt, until they come to the realisation of

The Journey to my Life Purpose

loving themselves. When people take on a three year it is quite a sensitive year for anyone who is not in touch with their feelings – like threes are!!

4. A number four person is all about everything being in order in life. They are very hard-working individuals, and it is generally hard for anyone, who is not a four, living with them, to make them sit down and rest. They do not handle change very well at all, and can be very hard task masters!! If you are in a four year you will generally have a very hard-working year, and will find it hard to move on in the year – its head down for 12 months.

5. A number five person is a very changeable individual. They tend to get bored with routine in their lives, always wanting to look at new ideas coming up and follow them through. They can also change their feelings about things "at the drop of a hat." When in a five year life is constantly changing, and this can be hard if you are the type of individual who likes everything in place and constant routine.

6. A number six person is all about the beauty of life, and the nurturing number six is similar to number three – in that they are both very sensitive people. All those sixes are extra giving and can overdo this to the point of making themselves unwell!! They are extremely kind people and do tend to talk too much.

Numerology

If you are in a six year you need to look after yourself more – step back from situations and look at life in a gentle way.

7. A number seven person is very spiritual and people living number seven are here to learn "trust and openness" because until they learn these two things, they find it hard to give back to others and interact with others from the heart. If you are in a seven year this can be quite negative, unless you have learnt some awareness in your life.

8. Powerful number eight is the infinity number and is a very lucky number. However, people who are living this number generally tend to live quite simply and don't look at the materialistic side of life. They are here to learn Abundance and Power. If you are in the eight year this can mean abundance for you, with money, power and travel on the horizon.

9. Number nine people are humanitarians, and tend to live a spiritual life. They are caring individuals and will seek work in the area of nursing, social work or humanitarian work. They do tend to procrastinate and put things off! When living in a nine year you will find it's the ending of a 10 year cycle, where you will be clearing things out of your life, anything that is of no use to you – including things in your mind!!

10. Please note there is not a Number 10 in the cycle.

The Journey to my Life Purpose

11. This is a Master Number and these people tend to live a somewhat over-the-top existence. They can easily be led by others. Mainly they start things but never seem to finish anything!! There is also a tendency for them to have a chip on their shoulder about most things, which leads them to being quite negative in their lives!! Master number years are not used by people other than themselves as when they reincarnate they come back again as Number 11 to finish what they started in a previous life.
12. This is a Master Builder number – Number 22 people are trying hard to achieve enlightenment, and like Master Numbers they come back to Earth time and time again to try to achieve what they didn't finish in a previous life!

To learn about your personality character number, you take the day of the month that you were born on (reducing it to a single digit if above 9). For example: I was born on 1 June – so number one is my personality character number.

Positive traits for me: determination, self-confidence, will power, dignity and originality.

Negative traits for me: stubbornness, willfulness, over-sensitivity, arrogance and lack of foresight.

Numerology

Early Life Cycle Number from 0 – 28 years

The Early Life Cycle number is calculated by taking your day and month of birth and reducing to a single digit. Then take the numbers of the year that you became 28, and reduce that to a single digit. You then add both of these single digit sums and reduce to a single digit. Generally, the number will be one greater than your life path number, unless your life path number is 9, and then your early life cycle number will be 1.

My Early Life Cycle number is 4 (1 + 6 + 1949 + 28), and the interpretation of this is as follows:

You were intelligent, patient and humanistic as a child, but your expression may have been stifled by a childhood filled with discipline and restrictions. It can also indicate early years that were filled with poverty or abuse. Usually a person with this number has to fight great arts to succeed, and often they do. The upside of this is that you have a stamina, empathy and self-sufficiency during this period that normally is not characteristic of others of comparable experience or age.

The Journey to my Life Purpose

Middle Life Cycle Number – 29 – 58 years

To calculate this number take your Early Life Cycle number and boost it by a number. For example, my Early Life Cycle number was 4, so my Middle Life Cycle number is 5.

The interpretation for Middle Life Cycle Number 5 is as follows:

You may feel a bit lost in life or like you are having difficulty settling down. You are an impulsive individual who is fated to go through a series of jobs and relationships. This is because you become bored very easily. You prefer a life that is full of adventures over security and stability and as a result break many hearts. You are destined to travel or pursue exotic experiences, simply to satisfy your endless curiosity.

Later Life Cycle Number – 59 – 85 years

To calculate this number, boost the Middle Life Cycle number by one, so my later life number is 6.

The interpretation of the Later Life Cycle number 6 is as follows:

Numerology

You are likely to be very content and financially secure. Your family and especially your partner and grandchildren become the most important concerns in your life. Chances are that you will become very active in your family life and act as a secondary provider to your own children. It is a 6 that is most likely to adopt a child later in life.

If you wish to learn more about numerology – I have found the best book to read is Dan Millman's "The Life You Were Born to Live". It is "A Guide to your Life Purpose" book which you would use more for reference purposes, to help you also become unstuck in your life – which we all do from time to time.

The Journey to my Life Purpose

- CHAPTER 10 -

Meditation

Meditation is very important in our day-to-day lives. A little meditation is better than no meditation. 20 minutes at least is recommended, but 10 minutes can still do wonders. Meditation allows your body to relax and recharge. It helps to take away stress, it's relaxing, and it gives you time to yourself. It relieves the mind from all the chatter. People who have a lot of chatter and say they can't meditate, need meditation more than ever. Meditation helps to stop the chatter, maybe not the first time but with practice it

The Journey to my Life Purpose

will quieten more and more. You may focus on a guided meditation to start with. There are many sorts to choose from. I like to get a variety as it depends what mood I am in. Find a quiet place, even in the garden. Actually gardening, walking, knitting, sewing are all forms of meditation.

So, find a quiet place, sit or lay down, it is important that you are comfortable. Be careful not to sleep. There is a fine line between sleeping and going into a deep meditation. If you do sleep, and it's probably what you need and you are relaxed anyway, you will still pick up on the meditation. Sitting is good because you have a straight spine and the energy can flow down. It's better not to sit with legs or arms crossed as this restricts the energy flow. Follow the person's voice if guided. Don't worry about thoughts popping in your head. The aim is to eventually not have many thoughts popping in, but this takes practice, so don't spoil the relaxation by worrying about not worrying. Just be. Allow whatever changes your mind to be there, and allow it to pass on, don't stop it and analyse it – just let it pass. Eventually all the things that you have done during the day will come and go – that is the idea, to let them go. Take three deep breaths and hold each for the count of four, exhale taking with it any pain or emotions. Fill the entire tummy area. On the next breath tighten the whole body as hard as you can – face, fingers, toes, tummy, buttocks – hold

Meditation

everything for a count of three and again release the last of any stress or pain with it. Breathe out a sigh or moan. Have no expectation with meditation. Just enjoy the quiet space and just be away, just observe.

Some people see colours, some hear messages, some have visions. Meditation helps with psychic growth. It's healing. It raises your vibration, you may interact with guides etc. Everyone is different and we are at different levels of learning and growth. Don't compare yourself with anyone else. We are perfect where we are at this very moment. Things won't happen before they should, so be patient.

You may wish to sit with music or sit in silence, just listen to the sounds around you and out of doors. Focus on your breathing; if your mind is busy just come back to your breathing. There are many ways to meditate – you will find ways that suit you. Meditation helps you to stay healthy. The more you meditate the more clearly you think, and the more aware you become. Meditation brings about balance and calmness. It enhances your psychic abilities. Live each day as it comes and…..be. Be guided by your heart and feelings. Trust the process of life. Trust that everything is happening for your highest good, even if you can't see it

The Journey to my Life Purpose

now. Live honestly – to yourself and others. Only do things that make you happy. Be responsible for yourself and have no expectations on others.

Love yourself and your own company and you will then have no need for anything. We are already whole and complete. We do not need anyone or anything to complete us, we are complete.

In a relationship, it is better to be whole and complete to start with, in possession of your own identity, own interests etc. You should keep it that way during a relationship, then, if the relationship parts, you won't be lost, always whole, always complete.

Enjoy love, life and share, but always stay in your power; we need all the energy we have. We are on different pathways. We need freedom and choice to grow.

Joining a class of meditation helps you to obtain the skill, and educates your body to relax and switch the mind chatter off. It can also help you to breathe in and out and signal to the body that you are going into a relaxed state.

Yoga is also another way of doing meditation with yoga exercise.

Meditation

Meditation can also help you to clear your mind so that you can concentrate much better, with less stress in your life!

The Journey to my Life Purpose

- CHAPTER 11 -

Reflexology

In December 2004, whilst I was working at Fremantle Hospital, I decided to do a short course in reflexology, which I felt would add quite well to my Reiki when healing others. I also found it was a very therapeutic modality that would help people relax much the same as the massage, before receiving Reiki healing. I have since found that it works best to give clients a choice, or else they can have all three modalities when coming to see me. Reflexology is a modality that is a form of compression massage to the feet.

The Journey to my Life Purpose

It helps nature to normalise body functions, and is a safe and an effective way to better health. The benefits are:
a) It is relaxing for the whole body.
b) It improves circulation/metabolic activity.
c) It provides relief to tired and aching feet.
d) It aids the removal of wastes.
e) It helps nature to normalise body functions.
f) It is a safe and effective way to better health.

Some of my clients who had this treatment found it helped them with conceiving their first child. It also helped some clients with menstrual problems.

I first started to use this modality in 2006, when I was given a message by spirit while practicing Reiki healing at the feet of clients. I was told to learn reflexology as it would help clients to become more relaxed before receiving the healing. When I started with my business in 2003 not many people were open to Reiki healing, so I offered back and neck massage to help them relax. Spirit ensured me that reflexology would give clients another choice, and so I went to the Australian College of Aromatherapy in Victoria Park, in Perth to learn this modality. I passed the exam in late 2005 and started practising it in 2006.

In the last year I've had to stop doing reflexology along

Reflexology

with my neck and back massage, as arthritic conditions have started to become quite painful in my hands. Instead of doing these modalities, I have offered a psychic reading with the healing, which helps the client come to terms with other issues in their lives.

The Journey to my Life Purpose

- CHAPTER 12 -

Psychic readings

In 2010 I started to take an interest in psychic reading work. That was the year we moved to Baldivis near Rockingham in Perth. Before the move date, I made contact with spiritual people who practiced in Rockingham. I firstly found work one day a week doing readings in a spiritual shop, which helped me to connect with like-minded spiritual people and find out about other businesses in the area.

In October 2010 I left the Spirit Beyond shop in Rockingham

The Journey to my Life Purpose

and found more reading work in Como near Perth. I travelled to Como from Baldivis on Tuesdays, Thursdays and Saturdays to do readings in a bookshop. This was fine and very enjoyable until March 2011 and then the business in the bookshop began to tailor off, so I decided to see clients in my own home, and from a room in Wellard, near Kwinana some of the time.

In October 2013 I did a Conscious Living Expo at Claremont Showgrounds doing psychic readings, and the same again in October 2014 at the Belmont Racecourse in Perth.

When doing this modality you need to learn about effective protection techniques for yourself. You need to learn how to surround yourself with white light protection. To do this effectively you need to ask for protection for each and every cell of your body. I do this by circling my body in white light completely from my head down to my feet, and then sending some prayers to the divine.

Protection Techniques
- Surrounding yourself with a white light.
- Prayer.
- Meditation.
- Lighting a candle.

Psychic readings

- Amulets or Talismans e.g.: crystals for protection.
- A crucifix.
- Flower essences.
- Burnings smudge sticks to cleanse the environment.
- Incense.
- Mirrors to deflect energy outside the home or business.
- Energetic/metaphysical symbols, e.g.: Reiki symbols.

If you plan to open to others please remember these steps:

Protect yourself – as above. Open up – become aware of energies within and around you – focus attention on the person with you. Receive and relay information – ask if he/she understands what you are saying, and obtain clarification if required. Close yourself down – close down your chakras, shift your focus away from the person before you, and back to yourself. Cleanse yourself – you might flush your body with white light, take a short walk outside, or if you have time, take a salt bath or a swim in the sea.

Connecting with spirit guides or your higher self through deep meditation doesn't always give you the answers you desire. When this happens it may be because it is not the right time in your life to be asking this question, because

The Journey to my Life Purpose

you are not ready to receive the answer; or perhaps you are not asking the most appropriate question. Spirit guides are simply people without physical bodies, who offer to guide or assist us in our spiritual development. These guides can often change as we change or move on, or in/out of our lives, on our spiritual path. You also need to make sure the questions you ask are specific and direct. If you are not obtaining the right answers to your questions it may mean that your intuition needs to be developed more fully. This is where you will need to look at some psychic development classes to help you develop your intuition, and improve decision-making. You want to have confidence about the results of your endeavours in life, before you commit to months or years of effort.

Basic tools for spiritual intuition:-
- Meditation, reflection or prayer.
- Yoga, or gentle repetitive physical exercise.
- Sports which are repetitive and require physical and mental agility, such as surfing or long distance running.
- Techniques to quieten your mind so you can hear the small voice within.
- Practising using your intuition at every opportunity – playing with it like child plays with an idea or a new concept.

Psychic readings

Spiritual intuition requires that you listen to your soul or psyche, to glean information from that part of yourself regarding which is the best path to take.

When you become skilled at using your spiritual intuition, you seem to be able to remain in the present, aware of your surroundings, and still be in touch with that part of yourself to guide yourself to a more fulfilling life. These rare people are said to be in a state of enlightenment.

Spiritual intuition requires consistent effort to develop, especially with the demands of the modern world. Good reliable intuition needs lots of practice. Be patient with yourself. When you test your intuition and find you get inaccurate or only partially accurate results, keep practising – eventually you will gain confidence in the accuracy of information you receive.

Angels and archangels

Angels have been around since the beginning of time and people all over the world believe that they have their own guardian angels and spiritual guidance. You do too!!

Angels, unlike humans, do not have free will. They work

The Journey to my Life Purpose

directly with and for our divine creator, and their purpose is to help protect us. Angels love to assist us in many ways. They help, and their love is totally unconditional. I suppose you would liken it to the way animals love you!

Archangels help others with problems that come up in our everyday lives. All we have to do is ask them for assistance through meditation or through having a psychic reading or just by asking them!

ARCHANGEL MICHAEL

He is the protection Angel, Archangel of the south and the element of fire – ask Archangel Michael to give you physical and emotional protection as well as psychic protection from confrontational situations.

ARCHANGEL RAPHAEL

He is the healing Angel, Archangel of the East and element of air. Ask Archangel Raphael to help you with physical, emotional and spiritual healing and any rifts in relationships which need healing. You can do this on a personal or planetary level.

Psychic readings

ARCHANGEL GABRIEL

He is the messenger Angel and very wise. He is Archangel of the West and the element of water. He will give you guidance on your spiritual journey for your future, if you ask him wholeheartedly.

ARCHANGEL URIEL

He is the peaceful Angel. He is Archangel of the North and the element of the earth. He gives peace to your heart and soul, and peace within the family. Planetary peace can be gained from Uriel too. Ask him if you can be a channel for God's peace.

ARCHANGEL JOPHIEL

He is the creative Angel. Ask him to give you creativity to act and speak in an enlightened way, he is the Angel of illumination.

ARCHANGEL ZADKIEL

He is the Angel of joy. Zadkiel will enfold you in the transformational energy of the violet flame, and transmute all your negativity into joy if you ask for this.

The Journey to my Life Purpose

ARCHANGEL CHAMUEL

He is the Angel of love. Ask for Archangel Chamuel to enable you to experience self-love and dissolve feelings of low self-esteem. He will also help you to find true love in personal relationships.

ARCHANGEL METATRON

He represents the judgement of the divine throne. Also he is said to be the overseer of the Angelic keepers of the akashic records.

Connecting with Angels and Archangels is a good way of starting to do Psychic work. I started doing readings with Angel cards and I still use them from time to time even now. I also find Angels help me with my Reiki Healing and they give me signs that they are around through music, finding things that I have misplaced, finding parking spaces, arranging meetings with other people on purpose. They also have helped me with my automatic writing, which first came to me when I was doing Reiki Healings, and they gave me messages regarding my clients. They used to give me all the messages at once, until I asked them to give me all messages at the end of the healing. I start to write and they work through me. I also find I do not need my glasses when

Psychic readings

I write at first, but after a while my sight will deteriorate and I have to use my glasses.

I do hope this information is of use to you if you wish to pursue a Psychic Reading path.

The Journey to my Life Purpose

- CHAPTER 13 -

Reiki Healing

To this year, 2015, I am still practicing my Reiki healing, along with readings and numerology, to help people through the anxiety common in depression, and when they are stuck in life.

The benefits of Reiki are that it: –
- Energises the body.
- Opens the mind to emotional changes.
- Brings awareness to dreams.

The Journey to my Life Purpose

- Detoxifies the body.
- Causes old/unwanted habits to lose their importance.
- Calms the mind and body when stressed.

I am happy to assist anyone who is willing to learn the modality. The levels are:

- Reiki 1 (Introductory level) - learning to heal friends and family.
- Reiki 2 (Practitioner level) - healing the public as a business.
- Reiki 3 (Masters level) - teaching others the modality.

Before I finish the writing of this book I would like to share with all my readers, the passion I have truly held in my heart from my Reiki healing. This has been a wonderful godsend to me, as I was a very anxious person during my early years of life. Learning Reiki here in Australia in 1993 was the best thing that I ever did. It is hard to tell people who have not experienced the joy and passion, but to try it is one step, and of course if it does not resonate with you, at least you have given it a go!

- CHAPTER 14 -

The end of my journey

Before I end this book, I wish to give further information to all those who are embarking on a spiritual journey similar to my own.

Firstly I would like to say that sometimes you can tell a job or activity is not going to help you on your true path – it won't be to your liking and you'll ask yourself "Why am I doing this?" All I can say is, continue to do it as a stepping stone to where you are going, because believe me,

The Journey to my Life Purpose

everything I have done in my life has been used to enable me to reach my life purpose or heart's desire. For example, the medical terms I learned when I was a medical secretary came in handy when helping clients. This didn't mean that I could diagnose – that is definitely a No! No! – but it helped me to understand clients and listen carefully, before helping them intuitively with the healing process. Likewise, the massage component of the course in beauty therapy taught me about the muscles and the bones in the body, which is also useful knowledge for a healer. Of course I also learned how to do waxing and nails etc., which I never enjoyed and never used professionally. It didn't matter – you actually take what you need from things you learn, and that helps you to fulfill your passion!!

I did quite an extensive counselling course in Transactional Analysis and I gained several certificates. Because of this I learnt how to listen to clients, and was able to help clients who didn't love themselves. The counselling training enabled me to teach clients to love the child within themselves. It also taught me that we humans play mind games and how we can stop those from happening!! I learned all about holistic counselling which is all about working with spiritual thoughts and helping people to help themselves through depression. Meditation, which stills the mind, and Reiki healing can also help people to beat depression.

The end of my journey

Becoming a healer helped me to understand my own bad experience of depression, after having twins and bringing up a three-year-old. The depression took a hold when I was 32 years old; I learnt that I needed to give myself 15 minutes each day, and my counsellor at that time (1982/3), also suggested I listen to a record of meditation and breathing techniques. Doing this made me realise that there was light at the end of the dark tunnel!!

I found the contacts that I made through my businesses seemed to help me have the confidence to progress more fully, and enjoy the interaction with people.

Just last year my husband and I went on a four month long trip to Canada and the UK to see relatives. I must admit it was a very long time to be away, but we wanted to see our new granddaughter Darcey and have quality time with her. After two months I was really wanting to come home here, and I guess that tells me that "home is where the heart is". Lots of people have asked me why I came to Australia and I always answer, "for quality of life". I certainly wouldn't change that big decision we made in 1987.

I do hope you have enjoyed reading my "Spiritual Journey" and I also hope you can glean something from the information I have passed on to you.

The Journey to my Life Purpose

I am very blessed that I have been able to follow my heart's desire and, with the help of my dearly devoted husband and partner, I followed that passion wholeheartedly. All it takes is to come out of the headspace (where the confused monkey mind resides), and go into the heart and gut feeling (stomach and solar plexus area), to experience joy and a passion for life – this is where you will find your "heart's desire". Oh what a feeling!! I hope with all my heart you find true passion in your lives.

Blessings to all,

Elizabeth Ann.

The Journey to my Life Purpose

Further Information

Elizabeth Ann has skills to train you in Reiki healing level one through to Reiki Master along with many other modalities shared in this book. You can find Elizabeth Ann on www.elizabethann.com or via email on info@elizabethann.com.

The Journey to my Life Purpose

The Journey to my Life Purpose

About the Author

Elizabeth Ann has been a healer for many years and had a desire to write to help readers gain a better perspective of the journey to each of our own life purpose. With more than twenty years of experience, Elizabeth has gained much knowledge on helping others move forward in their personal journey to live a purpose filled life.

Elizabeth Ann was born in England and resided whilst growing up and immigrated to Western Australia in her

The Journey to my Life Purpose

adult life. In Australia whilst working for the Fremantle Cemetery Board she became interested in spirituality. After qualifying as Beauty Therapist she found her niche in Swedish Massage and explored her interest in counselling skills completing a course in Transactional Analysis which gave her great insight. After discovering the benefits of Reiki healing, she studied Reiki 1 & 2 to combine with her Swedish Massage skills and started as a practitioner and later added Reflexology. Her repertoire of skills provides her clients with a very relaxing and healing unique experience. Becoming a Reiki Master being the highest level of training, has allowed her to also train others in this healing technique. With her spiritual healing and development, Elizabeth began passing messages through using her Psychic readings to enjoy the combination of all her healing skills one on one and also at psychic fairs, expos and parties.

Elizabeth Ann is also trained as a Civil Marriage Celebrant conducting marriages, naming ceremonies, renewal of vows and commitment ceremonies in her region. She recently retired from this as she wishes to travel.

Elizabeth Ann continues her work with her husband by her side and travels throughout Australia healing others on their journey.

The Journey to my Life Purpose

Acknowledgements

When I set out to write this book in 2012, I felt writing a book would be a relatively easy task to do. How wrong I could be! It takes dedication and support from those who are close to you to give you encouragement to keep forging ahead with your passion to write. I had been writing journals from 2004 until 2007 – these journals helped me to start writing about my journey.

Firstly I would like to thank my husband Peter who has

The Journey to my Life Purpose

been a wonderful support to me to put this book together, including doing the artwork for the front and back cover, which I feel is an inspiration for all those people who will be drawn to read it.

I would like to acknowledge my dear parents, in spirit, who nurtured me as a little girl into a beautiful lady, to reach out to all the positive things in life and never stop striving for the best in my life. I send all my love to them both and know they are both now together again and enjoying life! Thank you to you both, because if it wasn't for you, I would never have been able to follow this truly wonderful experience and journey. I particularly want to acknowledge the rest of my family for supporting me in my venture, my three wonderful girls, Louise, Amy, Julia and their respective partners Matt, Chad and Joel. Together with my dear grandsons, Ethan and Kaleb and my dear granddaughter Darcey, whom I love with all my heart, my dear sisters Margaret and Catherine for their encouragement, and my dearest friend Billie who has always been there for me in my life!

My spiritual and non-spiritual friends who have listened intently to me and given me encouragement on my path!

My publisher Liz Atherton, has been a wonderful mentor in the preparation of this book for publication, and has been a

The Journey to my Life Purpose

very helpful guide to me in all respects.

I would also like to acknowledge a friend and helpful author Karen Weaver who has written two books already, and read my first manuscript, giving me such encouragement to continue. This is a synopsis of what she wrote for me: "I recommend this book because through your story your readers can connect with your journey, and through your knowledge and guidance they can constructively implement it in their own lives."

I thank Karen very much for her help with her encouragement as I was able to implement her recommendations and apply them, by writing two sections Part A – "A Memoir" and Part B "Tips for Inner Peace" – a self-help section to bring my book to life.

For all the others who have touched my life along with the support of all the archangels and angels who have supported my journey...Thank you for your guidance and help along the way.

Love, Light and Blessings.

Elizabeth Ann

The Journey to my Life Purpose

www.ingramcontent.com/pod-product-compliance
Lightning Source LLC
Chambersburg PA
CBHW050539300426
44113CB00012B/2185